Making Data
Governance Work

Yvette M Desmarais

Technics Publications
SEDONA, ARIZONA

TECHNICS PUBLICATIONS

115 Linda Vista, Sedona, AZ 86336 USA
https://www.TechnicsPub.com

Edited by Steve Hoberman
Cover design by Lorena Molinari

First Printing 2025

Copyright © 2025 by Yvette M Desmarais

ISBN, print ed.   9781634628631
ISBN, Kindle ed.   9781634628648
ISBN, PDF ed.   9781634628655

Library of Congress Control Number: 2025936763

Carina, with all my love.

Contents

Introduction

Data Governance (DG) in large organizations can be daunting and complex. The variety of stakeholders, business groups, data quality issues, data repositories, and source systems combine to create an incomprehensible matrix of problems, projects, and potential focus areas. Modern organizations have many priorities, including increasing revenue, reducing costs, reducing risk, improving the efficiency of existing processes and systems, and reducing technology debt built through years of ignoring data and system issues or making business acquisitions.

Many books are available now to support data governance initiatives as data governance has finally risen to a priority status for organizational management and information technology leadership. I highly recommend that the data governance practitioner read a variety of these books, including "Non-Invasive Data Governance," the DAMA-DMBOK (Data Management Body of Knowledge), and other books. They will provide information on many aspects of data governance with which the DG professional should be familiar. Additionally, read everything you can on data management, data modeling, artificial intelligence and machine learning (AI/ML), data architecture, and other topics within the data realm.

Data Governance (DG) in large organizations can be daunting and complex.
How do we decide what work takes priority?

Even with serious self-education and data experience, data governance practitioners may find the extensive workload required for a data governance program to be overwhelming. We may be starting a new program from scratch or picking up the remnants of multiple attempts at organizational data governance. It is helpful to have a template with which to build a roadmap. This book will describe a hands-on process to identify, document, and rank data governance projects in a way that responds to the organization's needs while creating a practical, targeted, and measurable roadmap.

After establishing the roadmap, the data governance team and stakeholders can leverage the results to begin data governance activities across the organization. We then use the priorities and milestones identified in the roadmap to measure the success or failures of the data governance work. As with any system, these metrics should be used to redirect activities to the most successful paths or to reprioritize based on newly-identified risk and value-based targets.

To thoroughly understand an organization's data environment, we will build an approach to governance and conduct a review of the major data systems within the organization. This review includes an analysis of the various categories of risk and value opportunities related to data governance. We will rank each major system or data repository to identify risk and value opportunities. In addition to reviewing data risk and value, the review will document which data governance processes or functions are required to alleviate the risk and value issues identified for each data system or data set. Creating a matrix that allows the analysis of each data system by risk/value and data governance functionality will allow management to visualize and communicate the highest priority governance projects.

This book is for data governance practitioners of all levels of experience. I entered data governance through project management, business, and data analysis. Others, such as developers, SQL data analysts, or data engineers, come into the field with a technology focus. Still, other people come into the field from the compliance and regulatory side, learning about controls and regulations relating to data privacy. Finally, another route into data governance may be from the management and data enablement side, when a leader realizes the value of leveraging data across the organization.

Regardless of their initial interest in data governance, the practitioner can quickly become overwhelmed by the work required to control and manage data. You may find a different focus in each conversation with stakeholders in your organization:

- One team requires definitions and a data dictionary to understand data from a new acquisition.

- Another team needs data lineage for the data warehouse to use for reporting design.

- Operations analysts want a reporting dictionary with data lineage and transformation logic documentation to understand how reporting is derived.

- For insurance, the privacy department calculates the number of Personally Identifiable Information (PII) or Protected Health Information (PHI) records existing across the firm.

- Data quality issues have been a long-time issue in a legacy transactional system, leading to inaccurate decision-making.

- AI/ML data models need to be identified, documented, and tracked to manage risk.

- Incoming and outgoing externally shared data needs to be inventoried to limit contractual expenses and control data privacy exposures.

Where do we start data governance?

Where do we start data governance? This book evolved from my experience helping my employers attempt to grasp and organize the scope of work for data governance programs. The work can be overwhelming and composed of many small and large initiatives.

This book includes information about the wide variety of data governance functionalities and concerns, presenting some information about each area. This text does not cover all aspects of data governance but rather serves as a guide to finding an approach. Your organization may include some of these areas in other departments' responsibilities. For example, we can manage data privacy requirements and regulatory compliance within compliance, data masking and data access within a technical development team, etc. A data governance practitioner should understand how these functions relate to other aspects of data governance. Ideally, the data governance team is part of the decision-making process for these processes regardless of where they are in the org structure.

With AI and machine learning, our need for quality, controlled, and documented data will be more important than ever. This includes both the data going into AI/ML and the resulting data created by these systems. In addition to general information about data governance, the practitioner should study material on specific topics as they become important to the job. For example, one of my current focuses is on Master Data Management (MDM) as my organization is migrating from a legacy system to a new vendor. Understanding MDM as it could work now will help me support the move.

This book suggests a tactical approach to reviewing your current state data environment, creating an inventory of data sets, documenting today's challenges at a high level, and building a roadmap to data governance. Many organizations have started data governance activities where they felt the greatest need, such as master data management (MDM). For instance, a pharmaceutical research and development organization may focus on physician MDM. A financial institution might focus on client/customer MDM. Other organizations may focus on identifying and documenting systems, applications, databases, associated business owners, and technical managers. One organization I worked for spent years just documenting the software systems used within the firm. Unfortunately, the inventory has become overwhelming over the years, and there were few controls or documentation.

The approach I recommend leverages work that has already been completed within the firm, not starting over from scratch.

The approach I recommend leverages work that has already been completed within the firm, not starting over from scratch. That would be impractical and wasteful. I recommend getting a high-level, documented understanding of the current state. This should include asking about

- the what (what systems, databases, datasets),

- the who (people or organizational units that own or manage data),

- the where (software products and structures store and use data),

- and the why (what is the purpose of each data set) of data in your organization.

Learn and document the challenges related to data within your organization. Use the framework described in this book to evaluate and document the data governance challenges for each of your highest-priority systems and data sets.

Risk and Value

Two dimensions of data challenges relate to risk and value. Risk refers to potential situations due to loss caused by poor data governance practices, not following regulatory requirements, inappropriate use of data, poor data security, data quality issues, or other adverse events. This is the focus of traditional data governance. Value accrues when data is used to advantage within the organization. This may result from data analysts or data scientists finding insight from the data, creating revenue potential from data already managed within the organization, reducing costs by improving efficiencies in reporting or data processing, providing customers with valuable information, or other opportunities. This focus is often called data enablement and is a more recent focus of data governance activities. This book looks at both aspects of data governance. If your organization focuses more on risk avoidance or data enablement, spend time on these areas of the book.

Two dimensions of data challenges relate to risk and value.

Data Governance Functions

Another dimension of data governance includes the various functional elements of data governance. Because data governance is applicable across the organization and is 'all things data,' it has many types of work effort:

- data stewardship
- data cataloging
- business glossary compilation
- data quality analytics and measurement
- data standards
- process standards
- master data management

- data observability
- data privacy
- regulatory compliance
- data lineage
- data profiling
- AI/ML governance
- identity access management

Many of these relate to other information technology (IT) and business topics, as well as data governance, but they are all related to data governance as well. Look up data governance jobs on Indeed or LinkedIn for a few examples. Each job will focus on a specific aspect, but none will cover all of the above. This book will help you create a plan to encourage management to invest in data governance.

Another dimension of data governance includes the various functional elements of data governance.

Part I, Chapters 1-5, describes the aspects of data and data governance to include in a matrix to understand your data environment.

- First, compile an inventory of the most important data sets within the organization. Aim for directionally correct, not perfect. As time passes, the inventory will expand and become more detailed within each data set. In the beginning, a good understanding of the important data applications and content is the priority.

- Second, identify the high-level risks and value opportunities for each data set. Again, the aim is to document the most important aspects of the data, not every detail. Too much detail will result in confusion and less helpful information, as well as delays in providing value.

- Third, document the most important data governance processes or activities related to the data set. Yes, eventually, we'd love to have a full data governance structure for every data set in the organization, including named owners and data stewards, a full business glossary, end-to-end lineage, data standards with full detailed data quality reporting, on-demand data observability alerting, perfect master data management, etc. but that's not going to happen immediately. Nor do we ever have enough resources to do all this at once. So, prioritization is required.

- Finally, use the resulting matrix to select data sets and data governance functions to create projects and activities that will reduce risk and add value to the organization.

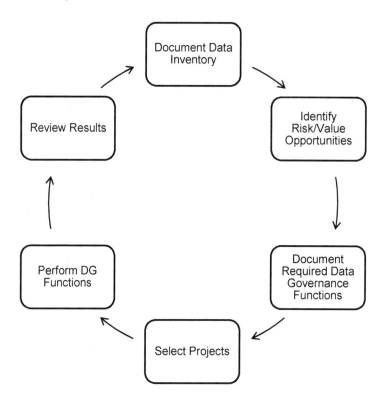

Part II, Chapters 6-16, introduces the functions that comprise data governance work. These include organizing roles and responsibilities, managing and reporting data quality, performing data stewardship activities, creating a data catalog, documenting and reporting on data lineage, and many others. Depending on your risk/value dataset matrix analysis results, you may or may not be interested in reading Chapters 6 through 16. Over time, you may need to include all these functions in your data governance efforts, but they won't all be the first priority. These chapters provide high-level guidance on the functions or activities, guide the practitioner in starting the work, and provide insight into the challenges and benefits of the activities. You will need to research further and apply this research to your organizational needs as time progresses.

Part III focuses on the ongoing activities that are an integral part of data governance. Chapters 17 and 18, covering Evangelize, Monitor, Report, and Evaluate, remind us that data governance work never ends. This may be frustrating to both practitioners and managers, but this reflects the expectation that data needs will always change as both the internal and external business environment changes and evolves. Additionally, it provides job security to experienced data governance professionals.

Caveat: For this book, I have focused on relational database systems (RDBMS) and the data within. These include industry-leading RDBMS products like Oracle, Microsoft SQL Server, Snowflake, Teradata, MySQL, etc., and industry-specific transactional systems that store and manage data in relational-type structures. These may include banking, retail, healthcare, and other systems that use either relational database systems or file-based systems that use files and fields. In some cases, they may use more complex file structures with multiple file types. However, I rarely touch on governance topics related to nonstructured data like social media, documents, audio, image video, blobs, web-based data structures, and other non-relational systems. The exception is relational columns incorporating large text blocks that create governance challenges. Practitioners interested in governing more non-relational datasets should perform more research into those areas.

The Data Environment

M odern organizations of any size use many different data sets. Even small businesses may use data from multiple systems, internal and external. Large, global organizations may use hundreds or thousands of applications, each of which may include multiple databases, database schemas, deployment environments, and data sets.

An organization may have one or more transaction-focused systems, a sales and customer relationship management system (CRM) such as Salesforce.com, one or more enterprise resource planning (ERP) systems like SAP, multiple logistics systems, inventory tracking solutions, asset management and tracking applications, content management solutions for managing marketing and documents directed at customers, research and development applications, master data management solutions for each high priority data domain (customer, product, location, etc.), multiple data warehouse/data lake/operational data stores/decision support systems, web-based systems providing direct purchase/ordering from consumers, etc. I'm sure your organization has many industry-specific applications that are not listed above, and this list does not include information technology used indirectly to run the business: email, intranet, security monitoring, service management, electronic messaging and connectivity, firewalls, websites, etc.

Large, global organizations may use hundreds or thousands of applications, each of which may include multiple databases, database schemas, deployment environments, and data sets.

Multiply the above list every time your organization acquires another organization or creates a new internal business unit. Even when acquisitions are moved to standard systems by the acquiring organization, some challenges arise due to the specialized nature of the acquired business. For example, a lab firm might acquire an organization focused on specialty testing. This business might not fit into the current architecture and will require specialized systems or data sets to support the specialized testing work. Add new complexity to the picture by incorporating artificial intelligence and machine learning (AI/ML).

These systems or applications create, store, manage, update, and provide data used across the organization. Most of these systems are linked in a complex web of connections, exchanging data back and forth between systems within the organization, collecting data from external organizations, and sending data to other external organizations. Consultants love to create spaghetti charts showing the complexity of the 'before' picture of data flows. Every organization has these webs, and they grow more complex every year.

Every system, application, database, schema, or data set may create data challenges that require data governance focus.

Data quality may be restricting your ability to understand your business at the level required, master data management issues may be creating problems with data sharing to non-authorized persons, inconsistencies in data migration may result in firefighting activities when data sharing to external parties goes bad, lack of data dictionary and business understanding of data may waste analyst time searching out the right information to create useful analytics, and inconsistent standards may result in design decisions contradicting regulatory requirements.

All these aspects are part of data governance, but there are so many types of issues, many systems, and many databases—where do we start? The following five chapters provide a guide to finding a practical approach to determining priority data sets, issues of risk, opportunities to create value from data, and identification of initial data governance functions. After completing the work described in these initial chapters, your organization should build a matrix identifying the best starting points for data governance activities.

Chapter 1

Data Set Inventory

The first step in implementing a risk-based data governance approach should be compiling a data set inventory. Many functions of data governance rely on understanding the scope of data across the organization. Prioritization of data governance efforts, therefore, will require an inventory of the data across the enterprise. This is not a trivial exercise, so approach the effort in a way that looks toward accuracy and suitability rather than completeness. When an organization has hundreds of applications running globally, it is not possible or necessary to document every data set. Focus on the most important datasets first. These will ideally be readily identifiable during discussions with business and IT stakeholders.

Organizations begin by identifying the highest priority applications, labeled with appropriate names (i.e., Tier 1, Crown Jewels, etc.).

The term *data set* identifies a collection of data within a given database or schema that addresses a specific subject area or process. The definition of a data set can be flexible and vary based on organizational needs. A data set will frequently encompass all the data from a given system or application, such as a system used to calculate and manage sales commissions. Or a data set may be a subset of a given application. This definition may be necessary for applications that multiple groups of people manage within the firm. For example, core systems store and utilize data from operational, accounting, billing, customer service, and logistical teams.

When organizational needs, data ownership responsibilities, or data governance concerns vary for different parts of a given system, the data sets involved should be called out separately. For example, when considering data within Salesforce.com, we might consider customer master data as a data set. This would include all customer address information, organizational hierarchies and relationships, contact information, etc. Within a healthcare provider organization, we might consider admissions, discharge, and transfer (ADT) information as a data set even if the ADT data is part of the electronic health record (EHR) that also supports ordering, pharmacy, tests, etc.

The level of detail for the data set inventory should focus on the known information about applications, databases, and data sets within the organization. For example, if the current focus of discussion for data governance is at the application level, such as Patient master data management, then that will suffice. If a large system, like Oracle's ERP (Enterprise Resource Planning), is used across the organization and includes functionality such as Accounts Payable, Accounts Receivable, Fixed Assets, etc., those functionalities might be broken out as separate data sets. Additionally, ownership might be a criterion for identifying specific data sets. For example, if the same technical and business leaders manage all the above ERP subsystems, they can be included in one line item in the inventory.

The data set inventory should include at least the following information:

- **Name**: A standard name as established in the most appropriate system of record. Often, large organizations use Service Now as a system of record for applications. This can be augmented with standardized names for databases and data sets.

- **Description**: A short description of the data set in question. The description should differentiate the dataset and application from other similar data sets.

- **Business Owner**: The business leader most responsible for the success of the processes that this data set, database, or application supports. This person will be responsible for ensuring that appropriate data governance processes are applied to the data set. This business leader is likely responsible for funding-related technologies.

- **Technical Owner**: The technical leader most responsible for ensuring that this data set, database, or application runs accurately, consistently, securely, and is maintained. This person will be responsible for ensuring that accurate technical information is provided and that data governance processes are supported for the data set.

- **Subject Matter Expert(s)**: The person or people who are the most knowledgeable about the data set, its uses, data challenges, interactions with other data sets and systems, and most appropriate uses. This person is often the most valuable resource for data governance activities related to the data set. It is important that their time is respected and any requests made to them are made as clear and focused as possible.

- **Alias(es) or acronym(s)**: Most applications/databases within an organization are referenced colloquially by one or more acronyms. Identifying those early can avoid confusion.

- **Deployment environment**: Development, testing, or production. Generally, data governance activities focus on production environments. Identification of the applicable environment will reduce confusion in future discussions.

Create the matrix using Excel, SharePoint, a database, or any other method you prefer. I've found Excel to be an excellent start. I recommend listing data sets on rows (at the left) with three main sections of columns: inventory attributes, risk/value categories, and DG functions. Initially, populate the matrix with text descriptions.

After drafting a preliminary list of data sets with attributes for the three sections, I suggest creating a column for risk/value with a numeric rating. You can fill this out any way, but a 1-10 or odd number system is standard. Odd numbers force the user to rank to one side or the other.

You may choose to add a couple of additional columns to rank Strategic Value and/or Readiness. These attributes can be higher priorities than other risk or value attributes. Strategic Value can be populated based on executive leadership priorities. Readiness helps to level set initiatives based on whether there are other projects or challenges related to the data set. Consider these when identifying project priorities. For example, if an application will be replaced or decommissioned in the next six to 12 months, there is no point in implementing a data governance process for the application.

Data Set Name	Description	Business Owner	Technical Owner	SMEs	Acronyms	Deployment Environment	Business Value	Business Priorities	Data Privacy	External Facing	Complexity	DQ Issues
PeopleSoft General Ledger	Contains financial information used to compile expense and earnings, management reporting.	Anne Bolin	Henry Tudor	Elizabeth Tudor	PSGL	PROD	9	5	5	0	7	3
ADP Payroll	Employee information for payroll.	John Smith	Edward Morris	Ben Best	ADP	PROD	9	5	7	0	5	7
FIS Core Banking	Customer transaction focused software for retail banking.	Dan Brown	Jodi Picoult	Franklin Pierce	FIS	PROD	9	9	9	9	9	9
Reltio	Master data management software used for customer MDM.	Freddy Mercury	Paul McCartney	Janis Joplan	RTIO	PROD	7	7	5	5	7	7
Moody's	Purchased data from Moody's for credit ratings.	Jane Doe	Joe Smith	Bob Smith	MOOD	PROD	3	3	3	0	0	5
MyBanking.com	Externally facing website used by bank customers.	Mary Pickford	Charlie Chaplin	Greta Garbo	MB	PROD	9	9	9	9	7	7

Therefore, your matrix should include the following (an example with a short list of data sets appears below):

Data sets/ application/ systems	Data set inventory	Risk/value categories	Risk/value ranking	Data governance functionality required	Optionally

- **Data set inventory attributes**: Data Set Name, Data Application, Description, Business Owner, Technical Owner, Subject Matter, Alias, and Deployment Environment(s).

- **Risk/value categories**: Business Value, Business Priorities, Data Privacy/Sensitivity, External Presentation, Complexity, Data Quality Issues, Data Knowledge, AI/ML Usage, and Organization Specific Issues.

- **Risk/value ranking**

- **Data governance functionality required**: Data Stewardship. Master Data Management, Data Quality, Metadata Management, Lineage, Data Privacy, Access and Entitlements, Privacy Classification, and Data Observability.

- **Optionally**: Strategic Value Ranking, Readiness Ranking.

CHAPTER 2

Data Governance Risk Categories

After creating a preliminary inventory, rank each data set according to data governance risk. This is the first ranking to help establish the order of approach for data governance activities. The following categories are examples of risk categorization. Modify your business value and risk avoidance categories based on the needs of your business, adding or removing those that are most useful. Rank value and risk avoidance. There are a variety of options for ranking. The simplest involves a limited set of numeric levels such as 1-5 (5 being the highest or most important).

Business Value

What are the highest-value data sets within the organization's data environment? For example, financial services include client accounts, transactional systems, and client-focused master data management systems. A healthcare provider may include billing systems, ADT (admissions, discharge, and transfer) systems, and order systems. A lab company might include testing master data management, LIMS (laboratory information management systems), and orders/results.

Interview management to identify evolving business priorities. Incorporate these in business value ranking.

Business Priorities

While it may be fairly easy to identify systems and databases that support the highest value to the business as a whole, priorities may change over time based on external circumstances, economic changes, or executive decisions. Frequently, business organizations work through periodic strategic analyses to orient enterprise goals to the current environment. Leverage this process to identify the highest current priorities for data governance. Many strategic goals in modern organizations will relate to data requirements in some way. For example, using artificial intelligence (AI) to provide recommendations to customers may require a focus on data quality for the underlying transactional database. Or, reducing risk by creating data governance practices supporting regulations around data privacy might suggest introducing assessments for GRPR and CCPA regulations.

Data Privacy and Sensitivity

What data privacy considerations are inherent in the data set? In the US, we see three major types of data privacy considerations: PII (personally identifiable data), PHI (personal health information), and financial or confidential information. These data privacy considerations have become an area of risk inherent in today's regulatory environment. Government entities focus on the exposure and use of PII, PHI, and financial data. Some governmental data privacy and governance regulations include HIPAA, GDPR, CCPA, and FERPA. An assessment of data privacy considerations should also include an inventory of the regulations that govern specific data sets. This will vary depending on industry and geography.

Health Insurance Portability and Accountability Act of 1996 (HIPAA)

US Federal law provides for "creating national standards to protect patient health information from being disclosed without the patient's consent or knowledge."

The Privacy Rule standards address the use and disclosure of individuals' health information (*protected health information* or *PHI*) by entities subject to the Privacy Rule. These individuals and organizations are called "covered entities."

The Privacy Rule also contains standards for individuals' rights to understand and control the usage of their health information. A major goal of the Privacy Rule is to make sure that individuals' health information is properly protected while allowing the flow of health information needed to provide and promote high-quality healthcare and protect the public's health and well-being. The Privacy Rule permits important uses of information while protecting the privacy of people who seek care and healing.

Reference

US Centers for Disease Control and Prevention. (2024, September 10). Health Insurance Portability and Accountability Act of 1996 (HIPAA). From https://www.cdc.gov/phlp/php/resources/health-insurance-portability-and-accountability-act-of-1996-hipaa.html?CDC_AAref_Val=https://www.cdc.gov/phlp/publications/topic/hipaa.html.

GDPR (General Data Protection Regulation)

The GDPR was introduced by the European Union (EU) and became applicable May 25th, 2018. https://gdpr-info.eu/

GDPR may govern your organizational approach to data privacy and control if your business works in the EU or provides services to customers from the EU. The intent of GDPR is to protect the personal data of EU citizens and residents. The regulation applies to personal data processed by or with automated systems and applies to data whether or not the data resides in the EU.

Reference

The European Parliament. Official Journal of the European Union. (2016, April 27). *General Data Protection Regulation GDPR.* From https://gdpr-info.eu/.

CCPA (California Consumer Privacy Act) and CPRA (California Privacy Rights Act)

The California Consumer Privacy Act of 2018 (CCPA) gives consumers more control over the personal information that businesses collect about them, and the CCPA regulations provide guidance on how to implement the law. This landmark law secures new privacy rights for California consumers, including:

- The right to know about the personal information a business collects about them and how it is used and shared;

- The right to delete personal information collected from them (with some exceptions);

- The right to opt out of the sale or sharing of their personal information; and

- The right to non-discrimination for exercising their CCPA rights.

In November of 2020, California voters approved Proposition 24, the CPRA, which amended the CCPA and added new additional privacy protections that began on January 1, 2023. As of January 1, 2023, consumers have new rights in addition to those above, such as:

The right to correct inaccurate personal information that a business has about them; and

The right to limit the use and disclosure of sensitive personal information collected about them.

Businesses subject to the CCPA have several responsibilities, including responding to consumer requests to exercise these rights and giving consumers certain notices explaining their privacy practices. The CCPA applies to many businesses, including data brokers.

Reference
California Consumer Privacy Act of 2018. From: California Consumer Privacy Act of 2018

Family Education Rights and Privacy Act (FERPA)

The Family Educational Rights and Privacy Act (FERPA) is a US Federal law that protects the privacy of student educational records. FERPA gives parents certain rights with respect to their children's education records until the student reaches the age of 18. This regulation requires that schools have written permission from the appropriate party to release certain types of information, that parents or students have the right to request record corrections, and defines what information may be shared in student directories.

Reference

US Department of Education. *FERPA. 34 CFR Part 99-Family Educational Rights and Privacy.* From FERPA | Protecting Student Privacy

External Presentation

Is the data set in question available to external parties beyond the organization? This presents additional risks not seen in internal data systems. Not only is externally available data more easily accessible to hackers and rogue players, but it also presents the risk of data quality issues becoming more visible to customers and other external stakeholders. The reputation of your organization may depend on the quality of data shared outside the organization. For example, an organization where consumers make direct purchases over the company website should have a consistent, complete, and informative catalog. Inaccurate inventory status, poor descriptions, and limited consumer search capabilities will restrict your customers' ability to use your site and make purchases. Poorly documented healthcare product information may incur liabilities if physicians select incorrect products or testing.

Complexity

Depending on an organization's industry and data environment, some data sets may be more or less complex than others. Often, this complexity relates to the business value or centrality of the data set and the organization's business focus. Additionally, complexity may drive, or be driven by, related risk categories like data quality issues or data privacy considerations. The most complex data systems are often master data management (MDM) systems. For example, healthcare providers may find patient master data management a complex and ever-evolving environment for data quality issues due to the need to strictly identify individual patients and secure individual patient results.

Data set complexity also relates to how a data set interrelates with other data sets. For example, an integrated data model for a healthcare provider might depend on five or more source systems with complex extract, transform, and load (ETL) processes. Or, a central transactional system may require multiple master data management systems to provide high-quality data for accurate information processing.

Data complexity can also relate to older, legacy systems that have evolved over time. We often see these systems in established organizations. These systems are often decades old and have not been replaced due to the centrality of their processing to the core business of the firm. For example, a bank supports a mainframe trade processing system running COBOL. Over the decades, many modifications have been made to add features to the trading system, and data has been extracted and used to create feeds for many auxiliary systems, a data warehouse, and dozens of clients. Unwinding this system may not be a priority. However, the data governance inventory must account for the data originating and managed within the mainframe.

Data Quality Issue Volume

An organization may begin its data governance journey at the point when large numbers of data quality issues have been identified. Some systems may be the source of most known issues. Rank data systems according to the number and complexity of data quality issues known to exist. Obviously, we will not know the specific number of data quality issues at the beginning of the governance process. But stakeholders will be aware of the general level of data quality challenges of systems.

Your organization may have been tracking data quality issues across a variety of applications or may have encountered some very visible problems caused by data quality issues. For example, reference data for a given data set may have become stale or obsolete over years of acquisitions and change. Examples might be the closing or opening of new customer facilities, changes in address or contact information for company locations, or mergers of vendor organizations.

What is the potential value of better-quality data in this data set? What have we tried to achieve and failed because this data set is of poor quality? Can we change the nature of our business if this data were more valuable?

Lack of Knowledge

Are we limited in using this data across the organization because we don't understand it? Could a data dictionary, data lineage, or other data governance toolsets improve our ability to utilize the data by providing knowledge? For example, some ERP (Enterprise Resource Planning) software products are built in languages that are not used by the analysts who need the data. A strong data dictionary could address this challenge. In the age of Agile programming, there is little documentation of data structures and ETL processing mappings. Data dictionaries and automated data lineage products can help analysts understand data meaning and sourcing. When an organization has a strong acquisition strategy, new systems may need to be integrated within the information technology environment. Subject Matter Experts from the acquired organization may or may not be available to help understand the details of systems in the acquired company.

Purchased Data

Another category of data to consider for data governance is purchased data. Examples might include reference data, data from vendors, or data from other related entities. Financial institutions may purchase reference data from Bloomberg, Moody's, Standard and Poor's, or financial exchanges. Healthcare organizations may purchase data about treatments, pharmaceuticals, reference data, provider master data, etc. Different departments within the organization may purchase this same data. Understanding and managing these contracts and data use agreements can save money by consolidating purchases, reducing the risks of utilizing data against contractual specifications, and canceling obsolete contracts. As the purchasing party, the organization may also incur a risk of disclosure of the third-party purchased data via data breaches or inadvertent data disclosures.

Shared Data

One area of elevated risk related to data usage is data shared outside the organization. Many organizations share data in multiple ways. A healthcare organization might:

- Sell de-identified treatment data with healthcare payors or pharmaceutical organizations,

- Share employee data with 401k financial institutions, health insurance payors, banking institutions for payroll purposes,

- Share result information with research organizations,

- Sharing sales data with marketing firms,

- Or share order information with other healthcare providers.

This creates many challenges when identifying and controlling data sets shared outside the organization. These challenges include managing regulatory requirements like HIPAA, CCPA, or GDPR related to sharing data, ensuring appropriate de-identification, tracking data sharing agreements and contracts, identifying ownership by appropriate team members, ensuring fulfillment of any exclusionary contractual or regulatory obligations, tracking any inadvertent data disclosures, tracking data breaches by third parties, plus all the other risks and opportunities presented with data created, managed, and stored strictly within the organization.

AI/ML Use

Using organizational data in AI/ML (artificial intelligence/machine learning) modeling creates an evolving risk to organizations. A modern data governance risk assessment would not be complete without showing how data sets are used in AI/ML implementations. When data sets are used as the basis for AI/ML models, the accuracy, understandability, and consistency of these sources become more important. If a data set is used as a major part of an AI or ML model, prioritize it in a data governance program.

Organization-Specific Risks and Opportunities

As always, your mileage may vary. Identify any risks specific to your organization, industry, geography, or other considerations that might be pertinent. For example, a start-up organization may not have data processes, governance standards, reporting, toolsets, etc. Standing up a data catalog platform may be a higher priority for such an organization. That initiative may help determine which data sets are the highest priority to focus DG efforts. At the same time, implementing data governance while implementing a green-field data repository or new transactional database may be easier than attempting to document a decades-old transactional system. Remember, it is not unusual for more established organizations to be functioning with heavy reliance on mainframe systems built utilizing COBOL or other 'dead' programming languages.

CHAPTER 3

Data Governance Functionality Requirements

The next step in your journey to making data governance work is to understand the various functions within the whole. Data governance incorporates all things data with a seemingly endless list of activities. It is important to scope a data governance program to include a reasonable work effort for the given organization, data governance team, and timeframe. This is part of the challenge of creating a successful or even helpful data governance program. Again, customize this list by adding or removing functions for the organization in question. I recommend identifying which data sets most need specific data governance functions or processes. In actuality, most data sets ultimately should be managed with many of the above data governance processes, but we need to be practical in planning data governance work. Management will not provide funding to attempt to accomplish everything at once.

Data Stewardship

Data stewardship refers to guided support of data quality and data improvement activities. These activities are often the first focus of data governance programs. For example, a healthcare provider might focus first on improving the quality of patient master data as the quality of this data is integral to many organizational priorities, such as patient data privacy and accurate billing.

We will not go into great depth on creating a data governance organization. Many other books, including the DAMA-DMBOK, can guide you in designing your data governance organization. My goal here is to enable the data governance team to approach the work in a practical and tactical manner.

Master Data Management

The need for Master Data Management occurs as soon as a set of data becomes big enough, important enough, or complex enough to cause challenges within the organization's data environment.

Two main types of structured data within an organization exist: transactional and master data.

Transactional data describes the actions occurring within the business. Transactions include purchases and shipments within a retail or wholesale organization; orders and treatments within a healthcare provider; orders, tests, and results within a laboratory or pathology company; product orders, manufacture, shipment, and delivery within a manufacturing facility; or treatments and visits within a physician's office.

Master data includes data about the people, organizations, places, and things that provide context to transactional data. People and organizational data include records and supporting descriptive information for data describing customers, purchasers, organizations, patients, healthcare providers, employers, healthcare payors (insurance companies), subscribers, volunteers, or any other parties involved in the business. Place data reflects information about organizational facilities, vendor locations, customer locations, etc. This data often supports logistical and shipping functions.

Master data about things often focuses on products or components of products. For retailers, wholesalers, and manufacturers, master data would include products and materials used to create those products. For labs and pathology companies, master data includes blood tests, tissue tests, genetic tests, urine tests, COVID tests, etc. Additional subject areas for master data may differ based on the business involved but might include locations, vendors, machinery and other large assets, or real-estate master data.

---

*One of the greatest challenges of master data is
identifying an individual, whether that individual is a
person, a place, or a thing.*

With patient or customer-focused master data, identifying an individual person is essential. In healthcare, HIPAA standards in the US, CCPA in Europe, and other regulations across the globe mandate the privacy of individual records. An organization must identify the correct patient to restrict medical record access to the appropriate people. Confusion can occur due to common names, similar addresses, multiple births, parents and children with the same names, and many other situations. Vendors or clients may be confused due to similar company names within or across industries.

Even if an individual person or organization is identified, their relationship with other people or organizations may be confused within data. For example, the current healthcare industry is rife with multiple business relationships, billing agreements, and other contractual agreements between physicians and other providers and provider organizations like hospitals, universities, and other organizations. While the US Federal Government has put into place the National Provider Identification (NPI) system, it remains a challenge to identify how specific providers are related to treatments and, thus, billing transactions.

Outside the healthcare industry, companies may have multiple legal entities that may contract with an organization in diverse ways. Financial services organizations often have multiple intertwined legal entity relationships within the organization, as well as with other organizations outside the organization. Understanding those relationships is important to keep an accurate Customer Relationship Management (CRM) system for sales, orders, and billing. Understanding geographic relationships within a customer organization can also be important, especially when working with sales territories and compensation calculations. Overall, it is essential to show both the individual master data entity and understand the relationship of this entity to other similar entities.

Master data management example

For a simple example of the need for master data management, think about your cell phone contact list. If you have not been consistent with de-duplicating your contact list, you may have multiple entries for friends, family, coworkers, vendors, or other people you have met over time. If you use multiple platforms, such as your phone for calls and texts, Gmail, or Outlook for emails, or combine multiple email accounts in your current contact list, you probably have about the same mess I do. Contacts may show different names for the same person, contacts with just a phone number, or just an email address and no name. Single names with only a phone number. The above covers many challenges organizations face when managing data sets such as customers, vendors, products, or other high-priority descriptive data.

A significant difference between master data management and other data management activities is the concept of the current state and change over time. Master data sets, such as customer contact names, addresses, etc., may change over time. For example, a patient may move, a physician may add locations, a vendor may change their payment address or an internal company office may close or move locations. Unlike transactional information representing a business activity, master data describes an entity that is created, exists, has changing information or attributes, and then eventually ceases to exist. The data process should account for all these "states" of being. They may or may not be recorded in the database systems.

Additionally, we can implement master data management to control and manage mistakes and issues in the data. This can be incredibly important in healthcare data sets where HIPAA, CCPA, and GDPA regulations control how data breaches and issues with duplication and sharing of individual and health records are challenges, as well as financial services organizations where Know Your Customer (KYC) laws regulate approaches to Anti-Money Laundering (AML) requirements.

In "Master Data Management and Data Governance, 2/E, 2nd Edition, Alex Berson and Larry Dubov describe several important business drivers for master data management. These include:

- Supporting business development, sales, and marketing processes,

- Improving customer service efficiency,

- Risk, privacy, compliance, and control benefits risk management,

- Operational efficiencies, including reduction of duplication, research effort correcting problems, and improving speed of activities.

Other benefits of good master data management may include:

- Increasing the speed, efficiency, and accuracy of billing the correct customer or patient.

- Avoiding risk to organizational reputation by correctly identifying the customer during interactions.

- Maintaining an accurate, complete, well-documented product catalog that describes only active and saleable products without including obsolete information or items.

- Supporting an accurate, complete, well-described list of locations, stores, or service centers for internal and external stakeholders.

Master data management consists of the processes and data needed to accurately collate a set of high-priority master data. Due to the temporal nature of master data, change management is a high priority for these data governance processes. Master data may be integrated from data sources across multiple systems, whether of the same type (i.e., sales and contact management systems) or from a variety of systems, including internal systems like call centers, transactional systems, online sales, or external sources such as purchased healthcare provider databases.

Master data management usually requires coordination of data integration from sources of varying accuracy, requiring match/merge rules, unmerge rules and processes, prioritization scoring for overwriting attributes, etc. However, MDM also needs to account for changes over time, identify the sources of data changes, and have the ability to report back in time. Regulatory and audit requirements expect some mastered data sets to be reportable for content that may have changed over time. For example, sales activities may be measured and compensated based on sales territories or customer lists assigned in the past. Current assignments may accurately represent how sales were assigned when they were made. I've learned from experience that sales personnel get prickly if their commissions aren't correct.

Data Quality

Data quality activities directly focus on data quality issue resolution for a data set. Introduce data quality initiatives at any point within the organization's data governance journey. For instance, a new project may begin with a data quality review of incoming data sets. This initial review will only review the relative need for data quality improvements by data set. Data quality governance can be another time sink.

While it's important to understand the process of data quality improvement, the details can be left for a time when the data set prioritization has been completed and individual data sets are in focus.

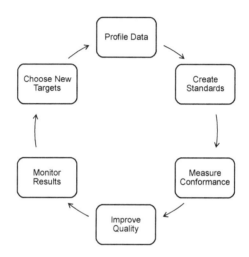

The data quality analysis approach recommended here includes the following steps:

- Data profiling helps us understand the data at the column level. Utilize SQL or more advanced data profiling tools to understand the content and trends within the data set within and across columns.

- Identify and document data quality standards pertaining to high-value or poor-quality data elements.

- Measure conformance of actual data sets to data quality standards.

- Apply data correction processes to improve conformance to data quality standards. This is obviously the most difficult and most important activity in data quality governance.

- Monitor ongoing improvements or degradations in data quality conformance to standards.

- Evaluate results and select additional data quality targets.

Data Cataloging and Metadata

The organization may find that making a data dictionary and associated metadata available to users is a high priority for certain data sets. For example, an organization may have implemented a large data warehouse, data lake, or another similar platform. Without a data dictionary, users may not be able to review the expected content of data sets within the data warehouse.

Many data repositories allow user access to various data sets, including integrated analytic databases and copies of data systems not readily available through standard tooling (i.e., mainframe, Cobol, or metadata-driven technologies). Security concerns require that engineers, analysts, and data scientists do not have access across such diverse data sets without proper request and approval processes. But, without the ability to review a presentation of the repository content, the request process can be inefficient and seemingly random. How often have we seen a development team send emails requesting, "I need data from X process. Do you know where it is?"

Metadata management can be an important component of data governance. Let's discuss the types of metadata that support various aspects of data governance.

Business Metadata

Business metadata usually consists of business language that provides the meaning and intention for data and data usage within the organization. Business metadata often starts with a business glossary, acronym list, definitions, and other information about business terms used across the organization. Ideally, we should integrate business metadata with other types of metadata to provide a holistic view of data that both business and technical stakeholders understand.

Complexities of business metadata may include similar terms used differently across the organization, different terms used to represent the same concept in various departments, or terms used generically to describe complex, often confusing concepts within the organization. For example, I've seen the term "legal entity" used to identify a specific location rather than a legally or taxable separate organizational unit. Over time, the term changed in meaning from a separate part of the organization to a generic term that identified a site. Sorting such business language can be a frustrating aspect of data governance.

Technical Metadata

Technical metadata includes information available in and reportable from databases, files, systems, and other technologies where data is created, managed, stored, processed, extracted, changed, and sometimes deleted. Basic technical metadata includes the names and descriptive information about software, databases, storage devices, tables, columns, files, fields, etc. For example, technical metadata about a set of columns might include the column names, data types, lengths, nullability, key assignments, relational constraints, etc.

Challenges in documenting technical metadata include inaccessible data dictionaries from legacy systems like those on main frame systems using COBOL programming language (often the most important systems in established organizations); a large variety of databases used to store, house, and manage data; complex data storage technologies, including those which are not instantiated in physical form, those created in a metadata-driven design where the physical tables don't represent the business information needed, and those housed in array-type structures; unstructured data including large text blocks or image, video, pdf or other types of formats; and the sheer number of data sets existent across an organization. One of my employers identified almost two hundred potential software systems used at the firm. Another, over 700 applications. A third, over 3,000. If each system included an average of one database or data set with 100 tables, we see how quickly the number of data sets can overwhelm a governance program. In reality, most software does not need to be cataloged, but many systems may include dozens of database schemas. Some can include thousands of tables.

Governance Metadata

Governance metadata includes metadata used to manage and govern data. This may include expectations about data quality, also known as data standards. For example, we may expect:

- That a specific column within a table always have a value or be complete,

- That for a given state of an ordered product, the order includes a delivery address,

- Or that a given column has a robust textual description rather than just one word or one character content.

Governance metadata should also include resource roles related to data, such as data owners, IT managers, subject matter experts, data stewards, and the like. Identifying the roles and assignments related to specific data sets allows catalog users to contact those people directly to ask questions about the data, make requests, or get involved in any related projects.

Process Metadata

Data Flow Lineage

Data lineage refers to the processes and paths by which data flows from the originating system to any other system within or external to an organization. As soon as data is moved from the system of origination, tracking lineage becomes a challenge. Modern corporations use an increasing number of technologies to move data from one system to another. Some movement involves direct database-to-database connectivity and movement between tables. Still, more often, data is extracted from a system into a file, a message, or some other format and passed along to another system that may or may not modify the format and content before introducing the data into a new data set. We can create Extraction, Transformation, and Loading (ETL) processes with many tools that may apply proprietary techniques to export, manipulate, and load data to a new repository.

As technologies evolve and become more complex over time, it is more difficult to track the path of data. Manually documenting the planned path of data movements is time-consuming and error-prone. As soon as we document a source-to-target mapping, it becomes stale as the development process may not be as designed.

Ideally, lineage should be self-describing rather than documented in requirements or after implementation. While legacy data movement technologies and more complex paths may never be machine-readable, the latest data governance and data lineage toolsets have added the ability to read data lineage from code to create self-describing maps between systems.

Process metadata describes processes both as designed and as they function. Data flow lineage metadata usually refers to process metadata as designed. We can illustrate basic lineage metadata as high-level data flow diagrams down to source-to-target mapping spreadsheets used to document field-to-field mappings of data flows, including transformation logic. The issue with manual documentation in spreadsheets is that it is almost always inaccurate compared to how processes are built, coded, and finally productionalized.

For that reason, more software products have come on the market that allow data lineage to be "self-documenting" from the code. Collibra is an example of one of the cataloging tools that has done a good job moving toward enabling extract of data lineage from some databases and extraction technologies to be displayed for analysts. Unfortunately, many data migration technologies, especially legacy tools, cannot be dynamically read to create the lineage. See the section below on Data Lineage for more about data processes.

---

1 https://productresources.collibra.com/docs/collibra/latest/Content/
CollibraDataLineage/TechnicalLineage/co_technical-lineage.htm.

Data Observability

Data process metadata also includes data as these processes function. We refer to this as data observability. Think of this as compared to how your dinner recipes are written versus how you end up cooking them. The recipe instructions state to boil the noodles for five minutes or to al dente. In reality, your water isn't quite boiling when you drop the noodles in. Or your pot boils over and you must pull it off the burner for a moment. So, the process took eight minutes instead. Observability provides information on what actually happened versus what was planned. In data, this could mean that one path in the data migration didn't run due to a network failure or a database join didn't work properly due to changes in the data and no records were loaded. Information about the actual running of data processes provides process metadata.

While many aspects of data governance presuppose data at rest, data observability is primarily about data in motion. Both are important to the goal of understanding and controlling data within a modern business organization. Data is always moving and changing within and across systems. From the moment a data record or element is created, it could be edited, deleted, transformed, moved to another system, trigger a process, extracted and transferred to another system or organization, or reported via one or more analytic and reporting solutions. These changes may or may not be tracked, analyzed, or governed. These changes may or may not be related to problems that could cause important data errors.

> *While many aspects of data governance presuppose data at rest, data observability is primarily about data in motion.*

As data moves through spaghetti chart processes within organizations, each step introduces the opportunity for errors, both small and large. If a server connection goes down during a data transfer process, an entire day's worth of data may fail to load. If your organization is contractually required to provide daily loads to a customer entity, that could trigger fines. Smaller issues may occur at the data attribute level. For example, a transactional business team may decide to stop requiring a particular data element in transaction processing. Several steps down the data lineage, an analytic team may have used that element to filter or group data. Suddenly, reporting shows most transactions where the element is Null. A small change, but lack of tracking results in unexpected changes may affect decision making if not noticed in a timely manner.

In "Fundamentals of Data Observability," Andy Petrella provides a helpful model for understanding data observability. His model includes Physical Space (server, user), Static Space (data source, schema, lineage, and application), and Dynamic Space (data metrics, lineage execution, and application execution). While other areas of data governance focus on the current state of what data exists in the Static Space, data observability focuses on the Dynamic Space. Good data observability reporting improves the ability to identify and resolve problems with data in motion. Petrella states that strong data observability practices can reduce data issue detection latency, improve data troubleshooting efficiency, prevent data issues, improve decentralized data quality processes, and complement data governance programs.

Data Usage

While Petrella focuses on data movements within the organization, another aspect of data observability includes how team members utilize, export, query, and analyze data. In today's cloud-based data systems like Snowflake, we determine costs by processing activities rather than strictly on storage volume. Before cloud databases, we based costs on hardware acquisition and support. These costs are now baked into database costs and billed based on processing time and intensity to a higher degree than storage alone. Cost is only one reason for paying attention to data usage.

Data exploration, reporting, and analysis levels can be important ways to measure the value of given data sets. For organizations with large analytic teams or many data scientists, specific data sets may be of more value than others. It, therefore, makes sense for more effort and resources to focus on improving data quality, timeliness, and content for these data sets. Some data sets may be less useful and therefore removed from data repositories.

> *There is little sense in maintaining processes to support data structures, processes, data quality, and reporting for data sets not used by the intended audiences.*

Additionally, data observability supports other aspects of data governance: data access, entitlements, and data privacy. Tracking and reporting access to important data sets can quickly identify infiltration and inappropriate employee access. You can use many vendors and tools to track access to data sets and report on various dimensions of usage related to sensitive data. These tools include Monte Carlo, IBM Databand, Informatica Intelligent Data Management Cloud, and Metaplane.

Data observability tracking, monitoring, and reporting are complex. These tasks intertwine with other aspects of data management, including support, privacy, security, and data governance. As Petrella notes, attempting to track every aspect of data movement would be impractical. Just as it would be impractical to run constant data quality checks on every attribute and every potential data quality issue for each attribute, it is impossible to create observability tests for every process and movement. One of the priorities of this book is to help the reader identify how to approach improvement projects for maximum effectiveness.

Data Privacy

While you can manage data privacy within a separate department in your organization, this aspect of data management is highly related to the other functions of data governance. Data privacy is also integral to conforming to regulatory requirements for GDPR,

CCPA, and HIPAA laws. The International Association of Privacy Professionals (IAPP) reminds us that protecting privacy is important for the same reasons other data governance controls are important: privacy is an ethical obligation, laws and regulations cover privacy controls we must abide by, poor privacy controls can create reputational risk, consumers and patients expect strong privacy practices, and emerging technologies like AI and ML create new privacy challenges.

IAPP references Generally Accepted Privacy Principles (GAPP) as a framework for managing data privacy:

1. **Management**: "The entity defines, documents, communicates, and assigns accountability for its privacy policies and procedures."

2. **Notice**: "Requires that organizations inform individuals about their privacy practices."

3. **Choice and Consent**: "Allows individuals to retain control over using their personal information."

4. **Collection**: "The entity collects personal information only for the purposes identified in the notice."

5. **Use, Retention, and Disposal**: "The entity limits the use of personal information to the purposes identified in the notice and for which the individual has provided implicit or explicit consent. The entity retains personal information for only as long as necessary to fulfill the

stated purposes or as required by law or regulations and thereafter appropriately disposes of such information."

6. **Access**: "The entity provides individuals with access to their personal information for review and update."

7. **Disclosure to Third Parties**: "The entity discloses personal information to third parties only for the purposes identified in the notice and with the implicit or explicit consent of the individual."

8. **Security for Privacy**: "The entity protects personal information against unauthorized access (both physical and logical)."

9. **Quality**: "The entity maintains accurate, complete, and relevant personal information for the purposes identified in the notice."

10. **Monitoring and Enforcement**: "The entity monitors compliance with its privacy policies and procedures and has procedures to address privacy-related inquiries, complaints, and disputes."

Reference

Capple, Mike and Shelley, Joe. (2023) CIPM Certified Information Privacy Manager Study Guide. Sybex.

Entitlements and Access

Entitlements refer to how users are allowed access to data within the organization. Again, manage access controls and identity management in separate parts of the organization from data governance. Still, a strong data governance organization should consider access controls and identity management as part of their knowledge base. These teams should work together to ensure the right people can access data at the right time. Regulations like GDPR, CCPA, and HIPAA refer to the organization's responsibility to ensure that only appropriate people can access PHI and PII.

Privacy Data Classification

Privacy data classification refers to the activity of classifying data, whether in the form of document files, emails, non-structured data, data sets, data elements, or databases, in terms of whether the data includes sensitive data types. At a high level, these data types might include:

- **PII**: Personally Identifiable Information that might be used to identify or provide information about a person, whether this person is a customer, patient, employee, vendor, user, or some other individual related to the organization.

- **PHI**: Protected Health Information that might be used to identify or provide information about a patient, subscriber, or other individual with health or medical information within the data. This information is particularly sensitive and is covered by regulations such as HIPAA in the US and GDPR in the EU.

- **Proprietary and Confidential Information**: Information and data about the organization or organizations involved in producing, managing, or controlling the documents and information the data reflects. Proprietary information may include legal, corporate, marketing, research, technology, or other information important to managing and maintaining the business.

- **Non-Classified**: Information that is otherwise not classified as sensitive or confidential. This data may be generally available outside the organization and does not need to be specially monitored or controlled.

Accurate identification and classification of documents and data across the organization is a high priority in the process of controlling breaches and ensuring appropriate access and entitlements. Data Privacy classification can be used in automated toolsets to monitor email exchanges between employees and external parties to restrict and reduce inadvertent data disclosures.

Data Products

Many organizations have moved toward a data product focus such as that described by Zhamak Dehghani in "Data Mesh." In Chapter 3 of this book, Dehghani focused on the "Principle of Data as a Product." This idea focuses on the business value of data sets as useful, validated, accessible products that can add value to a business organization. The data product mindset provides a way to describe and discuss data with business stakeholders in a way that goes beyond the technicalities of database structures, lineage, design, storage, and access.

Data products can be targeted toward internal consumers, adding value by leveraging the existing processes, systems, and movement of data, or they may be targeted at external stakeholders in a way that could create monetized value for an organization. Think, for instance, of the healthcare organization that makes it easy for consumers to order testing or request pricing on services for comparison shopping. If your organization is interested in implementing a data product strategy within your data governance systems, note which data sets may be sources for data products. You may already have data sets that are informally considered data products.

Reference

Dehghani, Zhamak. (2022). *Data Mesh: Delivery Data-Driven Value at Scale.* O'Reilly Media, Inc.

Petrella, Andy. (2023). *Fundamentals of Data Observability.* O-Reilly Media.

Other Considerations

Other considerations in ranking target data sets for governance activities include:

- **Readiness**: Is the organization responsible for the data set able to focus on data governance activities? Does it make sense to look at these now? For example, spending a lot of effort analyzing data quality for end-of-life systems doesn't make sense, except to avoid replicating issues in the new implementation.

- **Strategy**: Is the data set in question part of executive management's future-facing strategy? Is the data involved a high priority to the organization as a whole?

- **Governability**: Some data sets might be important to the organization, utilized highly, and have poor data quality, but the organization may not have any ability to influence the quality or usefulness of the data in question. This can often be the case for data sets acquired from external sources. Some examples of industry-leading data providers are Discovery Data for financial services data and IMS Health (IQVIA), which provides data to the pharmaceutical industry.

Guidance for Risk Assessment and Prioritization

- Don't take forever to determine risk/value and data governance information for the data set inventory.

- Get a high-level understanding of the complexity and ranking of your systems.

- Identify the highest priority data sets. Even the largest, best-resourced organization cannot focus on data governance activities for all systems.

- Identify the highest value targets and place early focus here. Over time, you can add data sets as the most important ones to gain data governance maturity as acquisitions occur or as new data systems are added to the environment.

- Don't spend more time thinking about the process than making strides in governing and enabling data.

CHAPTER 4

Data Governance Challenges

U p to this point, we have identified most of the high-value or high-risk data sets across the organization, the major risk categories for each of the high-priority data sets, and the most important data governance functions related to the high-priority data sets.

Now that we have a fair understanding of the current state of data governance needs within the organization, it is time to start identifying projects. Do this in coordination with the other teams within the organization. Other books, like the DAMA-DMBOK, identify appropriate stakeholder groups within the organization who should be part of the conversation. Here, I'll identify work efforts, projects, and programs to create a roadmap for data governance efforts.

While you should conduct this inventory and prioritization at the beginning of a data governance journey, you should periodically update or repeat the process. Data governance is an ongoing process that is never "done". Data governance is a process of continuous improvement. Internal and external changes occur, which affect organizational priorities. Systems are changed or decommissioned, businesses are purchased and sold, markets arise or decline, and leadership makes decisions that affect how data is utilized within the organization. These will change how data governance is enacted and how data enablement practices are leveraged to improve the organization's profitability and growth potential.

Different organizations may be able to dedicate various resourcing levels to the data governance effort over time. For example, a data governance team may consist of one or a handful of team members focused on a portion of the organization, like one data repository. An organization may also have a larger, centrally located business team working under the compliance organization. Organizations may divvy up governance work across a variety of teams. Data Privacy may be part of an IT security team or part of compliance. Data governance teams may be scattered across a large global organization.

This book suggests an approach that applies to any size organization by using the data set inventory to identify projects and scale work to fit available resource levels. Once the team has identified the highest priority data sets and matched them with the priority data governance functions, break the effort to resolve issues, reduce potential risk, and create value by implementing data governance capabilities into project-sized chunks.

Data governance work has characteristics that make it difficult to organize projects or utilize Agile methodologies. Achieving any success in data governance requires the participation and cooperation of stakeholders across the organization. This creates a variety of challenges, one of which is that we may extend the timeframe required for accomplishing data governance target results due to the prioritization of other work by stakeholders and their management chain. This dependency can often delay the completion of projects in ways that can be frustrating for a dedicated data governance team.

Therefore, when you identify projects and plan timelines, you must consider the timelines of other stakeholders. You may need to allow extra time for non-Data Governance staff to participate, review, and contribute to these efforts. You may need to reduce the scope of data governance projects. One approach is to coordinate efforts with other teams to achieve aligned results. If your organization is building a new data repository, use this time to organize and document the data dictionary or leverage the new toolset to report on data flow lineage. Data governance and data enablement is part of many initiatives across the organization.

A similar approach is to co-opt stakeholder teams to achieve goals that support their needs. For example, an application team may need to understand all incoming and outgoing data flows to prepare for a major upgrade or system replacement. Coordinating their work with documentation of data flow lineage will serve multiple ends.

In Chapter 11, "Data Governance Tools – Common Data Matrix" of "Non-Invasive Data Governance", Robert Seiner provides excellent examples of projects and techniques for identifying work efforts. His approach differs from the one I recommend here but is equally valid. The point is to approach data governance in a way that works for your organization and adds value by either leveraging data to support organizational strategies or reducing organizational risks.

Reference

Seiner, Robert S. (2014). Non-Invasive Data Governance: The Path of Least Resistance and Greatest Success. Technics Publications.

DAMA International. (2017). DAMA-DMBOK: Data Management Body of Knowledge. Second Edition. Technics Publications.

People

Data governance project success requires the participation of multiple stakeholders, including data owners, application business owners, IT application managers, IT application staff, data management platform staff, IT project teams, and frequently Subject Matter Experts (SMEs). Data governance work may proceed to some degree with limited resources but can only be successful with participation from across the organization. Stakeholders such as those listed above need to participate in providing information for data governance activities, conform to requirements identified to support regulatory controls, utilize data governance systems, support data quality improvement projects, utilize master data management, and ultimately utilize the data created within the organization to make operational, tactical, and strategic decisions based on high-quality data.

Additionally, stakeholders must utilize the information gathered by data governance activities to enable the value of data. We cannot truly become a data-driven organization without communication and evangelization of data value across the firm.

SMEs are one of the most important stakeholder groups for data governance initiatives.

SMEs are one of the most important stakeholder groups for data governance initiatives. They are the people who know the most about a particular application, data set, or system. They are the "go to" people who are often the busiest in the company. They may have been with the organization for years or decades. Or they may have built the systems or been working in a specific department for long enough to know "everything" about the data.

An example might be the analyst who started in the call center just after school and has worked her way up to managing the patient master data management system. Or the data analyst manager who has been in a variety of departments for 40 years. SMEs are of high value to an organization because they not only know what is in application databases, but also know enough organizational history to know why the data is the way it is.

Business and IT application owners are another group that is critical to the success of data governance initiatives. These management owners have day-to-day responsibility for managing systems, making budgeting decisions, and directing staff members in prioritizing work initiatives. Application owners must support data governance efforts related to the systems they are responsible for.

You can utilize a variety of methods to gain support from stakeholders, including SMEs and application owners. Data Governance is much like project management in that we need to solicit help from many stakeholders who do not directly benefit from the project. Nor do we have direct organizational authority to force cooperation. Stakeholders in the organization usually have other jobs that are of priority before data governance activities. When requesting support, information, and time from other teams, we must consider these responsibilities. Over time, I have identified a few ways to obtain support.

The most important activity in data governance work with stakeholders is communication.

Approach this in a variety of ways. As Jay Conrad Levinson noted in "Guerrilla Marketing," it can take over 16 times for a consumer to see information about a product before acting on a solicitation. While we may not require that much communication, we need to be diligent about data governance communication before we can expect stakeholder buy-in. The initial introduction of data governance ideas may come from executive communications. Additional sharing of data governance should occur using other channels, such as the internal intranet, email communications, "lunch and learn" activities, and more. Subsequent communications can include departmental meetings introducing stakeholder groups to data, the data governance team, initiatives, goals, and projects.

Utilize a variety of approaches, including demonstrations, reporting quality improvement gains with metrics, illustrations of data lineage, sharing data catalog content, etc., varying the media as well as the channel of communication. Most importantly, though, one-on-one or small group meetings are extremely valuable in achieving rapport with stakeholders. These meetings enable the governance team to speak directly to stakeholders, describe the plans, identify goals and benefits or risk avoidance of the work, and listen to stakeholders, directing discussions to the aspects of data governance that most affect the people in the quest. This approach also 'co-opts' stakeholders into providing both goals and support to the effort.

Listening is key to driving success with these initiatives. The impetus of data governance activities may start with requirements to support compliance and reduce risk but the true value can only be achieved by also focusing on the benefits of data enablement. We can force staff to comply with requirements, but stakeholders need to buy into data governance initiatives to achieve the best results. Organizational behaviorists used the phrase "co-opting" to describe the act of getting someone to buy into an activity, even if somewhat against their will. If you can convince stakeholders that it is in their best interest or the organization's overall interest to participate, they will more readily help the process.

During these direct meetings, it is important to provide details about the given initiative, not just describe it at a high level.

- What exactly do we want from the team in question? Do we need a list of their business terms and definitions?

- Do we need help in identifying the meaning of a set of tables and columns?

- Do we need their help connecting the data catalog tool to their database?

- Do we need help understanding a process that moves data to, from, or through their systems?

Be specific, include timelines, and communicate the purpose of the requests. What benefit or risk reduction will they create for the organization? What benefit could it create for the team in question? Ask for their input and take that input seriously. Identify the next steps. Follow through on the next steps. Communicate results. Don't obtain help from a team and never speak to them again. If a team or individual has been more helpful than most, send a note to his or her manager. Mention it to your manager. Every small effort to encourage participation can be helpful. Remember the 16-contact idea.

Example of approach

An example of this type of approach is the work I've done with data scientists. I noticed they were utilizing our data catalog. So, I contacted them to discuss their needs and understand how they used the catalog. During those interactions, I encouraged their use of other aspects of the catalog. I also elicited information about what other content they might need. This team often used the catalog to look at data structures in our Snowflake data repository to find data sets for a variety of projects. I also asked the data scientists for information about the meaning of various data sets. They, in turn, provided guidance on the importance of data lineage work we did within both Snowflake and our ETL tool, Matillion. Once we built some lineage examples, we returned them to the data team to determine their value. This back and forth is extremely valuable in creating data governance solutions within a complex data environment.

Reference

Levinson, Jay Conrad. (2007). *Guerrilla Marketing*. Houghton Mifflin.

Time and Complexity

Other significant frustrations for data governance initiatives in modern, complex organizations are the twin challenges of time and complexity. As noted at the beginning of this book, data governance covers many aspects of the data environment, and many systems, databases, data flows, and connections. Because of this complex environment and limited prioritization of stakeholder time, data governance activities can take a lot longer than management and the data governance team would prefer. It may be possible for a small data governance team to perform work on their own, but normally, this is not possible. Other teams are required to help.

Example of approach

A short example will help illustrate this challenge. During one project, I was responsible for interacting with many potential application business owners. I needed to ask for the names of source system owners, document these, and obtain an agreement on ownership. This activity often involved multiple implementation teams who used a large variety of data sets from across a multi-national, multi-system, multi-entity organization. It was difficult to identify the source systems in question, contact potential business manager-owners, set up meetings and explain the project, obtain oral agreement, communicate with data governance catalog team members, and finally document the new owner's names. This is all multiplied by several dozen project teams. Just setting up meetings to make contacts and communicating the "ask" required weeks to find time on people's calendars. This was when the work went smoothly. When stakeholder managers refused to cooperate, it became more frustrating. When systems were orphaned by organizational change, it was worse. Ultimately, it all got done, but patience was important during those months.

Project Variety

A third challenge within the data governance environment is that data governance projects can vary in size, scope, and complexity. This makes it difficult to organize long-term goals and objectives, understand the required resource allocations and duration for projects, and plan for the unknown. In data governance, especially in the data stewardship functions, it is very difficult to know what issues will arise.

Example of approach

For instance, on one team, we had a new data steward who documented known issues in her subject area, which was company location. She went to each team identified as working with the master data involved and was able to list over 150 data issues, change requests, or concerns from stakeholders of the subject area. Some of these requests were small, like adding a new value to the drop-down menu for an attribute. Some were much more complex, like documenting and controlling the process of closing out a location. In some cases, the request or issue size would not be known until further analysis was completed.

We also know that some data governance processes may take many months or even years to bring value. Therefore, it is important to scope out intermediate goals which can provide value. This allows the team to show progress, provide stakeholders with capabilities along the way, allow management to measure success, and provide leadership with the information required to justify funding for longer projects.

An example of a project that might take months or years is creating, documenting, and providing online access to data lineage. We will explore this topic more in later chapters. But, as many organizations have evolved over years or decades, the complexity of data movements within and external to the organization has also evolved. Multiple technologies have been used to move data. These could include direct database-to-database connectivity, extracts of flat files such as CSV, XML, JSON, or text, messaging systems sending one message at a time as real-time transactions occur, batch file processing, etc. Programming languages and software tools, including Cobol, java, python, ETL tools, etc., may also vary. Few data systems can read data extraction, transformation, and loading code. The few that concentrate on the most modern, easily readable formats and code ignore those legacy technologies that older companies used to build some of their most important systems. While this work continues and more data catalog vendors include good lineage readers, it may take significant time and effort to truly document end-to-end lineage within a complex, mature company.

CHAPTER 5

Creating the Roadmap

As described in Chapter 4, Data Governance projects may range from small efforts of a few hours to larger work efforts lasting months or years. While Agile development process tools are used to drive technology work within many organizations, these tools may be hard to implement for data governance work. As stated earlier, data governance work efforts are not easily broken down into story points or specific hours of work effort. While some activities, such as introducing new data sets to the catalog environment, may consist of sequential steps, other data governance efforts do not. The investigative nature of data stewardship and data quality work means that we don't truly know how long something will take until we are close to finishing. Nor do data governance projects, tasks, or work efforts easily fit into the waterfall or Software Development Lifecycle (SDLC) method of project planning. These work efforts don't easily break down into planning, designing, building, testing, and deploying phases. They are more akin to developing business intelligence or data visualization activities, being very iterative and evolving. This type of work requires interactive development, stakeholder and user reviews, and further change and refinement. This sometimes looks more like Agile development than the SDLC.

Recommended Approach

Overall, I recommend a timebox approach to data governance planning and project management. This allows us to investigate the next few quarters or months and identify given goals. These goals may include several smaller initiatives or a limited number of larger work efforts. Goals can be more explicit and detailed for the next two to three quarters, and at a higher level for future quarters. This approach leverages an Agile approach without the detailed rigor of creating story points and measuring burn-down rates.

For example, a data stewardship team may review the existing list of data quality issues and change requests, prioritizing a number of these for the next quarter. Once completed, add more from the backlog. If you cannot complete all of them during the quarter, then some may need to be moved back into the backlog.

In another example, if the data governance team is working on data lineage, the quarterly goal may be to read lineage from the highest priority, most accessible source. In one case, we read lineage from the Matillion ELT between database structures in Snowflake to the Collibra data catalog. This actually took much longer than a few quarters due to changes in the Collibra process and challenges within our organization. This illustrates the importance of flexibility in planning based on the reality of work progress.

In addition to planning quarterly, I recommend running multiple initiatives concurrently. These should include both longer, more complex initiatives and smaller, more focused work efforts. This allows the team to continue providing stakeholder value while building the foundation for higher leverage improvements. For example, identifying individual data quality issues, finding root causes, and rectifying problems must often be accomplished one problem at a time. However, creating a system that allows data quality measurements, data observability reporting, and trending of data quality compliance can provide the basis for enterprise-wide data quality issue identification. It's like putting out fires individually versus creating an environment where fires don't start.

Do something to get the ball rolling. Over the years, I've spent many hours in meetings repeatedly discussing what seemed like the same details. This can often occur in meetings related to creating policies, planning processes, defining roles, identifying issues, attempting to solve problems, etc., all of which are required within data governance disciplines. Even when things are going well, there will be enough nay-sayers to inject negativity and challenges into the process. It's better to present drafted documentation, begin a data dictionary, perform some analysis, or get started in any way than to talk about each aspect of governance too long. Most aspects of data governance are easy enough to change, and change will not create failure for the entire program. Some choices, like choices for data catalog or data quality platforms, can be expensive and harder to reverse. However, we can leverage even those investments, metadata, processes, and learnings for future implementations.

What will become a failure is "failure to start." Many organizations may, internally or through consultancies, spend months or more than a year creating an organizational structure while not accomplishing any governance. Organizational structures, strategies, missions, and goals are great to see on PowerPoint and can help organize the various stakeholders, but ultimately, we need to govern the data. We need to provide access to users, provide information on what data exists in the organization, improve the quality of our data, track it through the various flows, identify where external data is sourced, document where our data is used—all that good stuff. Spending hours fighting politics about the final definition of a "data owner" will not accomplish these tasks.

PART II

Data Governance Functions

The core of this book will provide the data governance practitioner with a short guide to each of the many functions within the realm of data governance risk management and data enablement. These chapters will provide high-level overviews of topics including organization of the data governance team, data quality analysis and improvement functions, data stewardship programming, data cataloging, master data management, data lineage, purchased and shared data, AI/ML stewardship, regulatory data governance, and privacy, access and identify management. I've included these topics based on my experience in information management and data governance over the past 40 years. Each has appeared in some form throughout my career working with data. I'm providing these overviews based on more recent research to provide a light overview. If you find that one of these areas is important to your position in data governance, I encourage you to review the appropriate chapter, find more recent information on the topic, and dig deeper. Many books, experts, vendors, and other sources can provide much more in-depth information than I can provide here.

> *Start your analysis, document high-level goals and processes, document the "known knowns," and start working rather than attempt to identify every potential deviation off the "happy path" before starting.*

CHAPTER 6

Data Governance Organization

Several books have recommended approaches for designing the data governance operational model and associated organizational structures. Many organizations get stuck in this stage of the process. Creating a data governance operating model, identifying roles, creating teams and councils, etc., is important. However, an organization can get bogged down in talking about roles, attempting to define each to the nth degree, and trying to define the team for every contingency. In my experience, creating and modifying a basic model as needed to fit the organization is the best approach. Just as every company, nonprofit, and educational institution has different goals, leadership, communication styles, and needs, so will each data governance framework. We'll need to understand how data governance fits within the organization before defining the framework in its 'final' form.

Additionally, as we dive into governance projects and activities, we'll find out new things that were unknown to date. Just as development and business intelligence projects have moved to an Agile way of implementing technology, so must we move data governance to a more flexible approach. This is not to say there aren't basic organizational constructs to consider. We will investigate the standard recommendations here, but please refer to some of the recommended readings for more detail. The following are based on the model recommended in DAMA-DMBOK. Names of roles and committees may differ across organizations. The data governance organization may be centralized, replicated across multiple business units, or federated with a centralized data governance team that guides business unit teams.

Data Governance Steering Committee

As described in DAMA-DMBOK, the Data Governance Steering Committee is the highest authority within the organization for data governance. This group is responsible for creating a data governance strategy, high-level decision-making, and procuring funding for data governance activities. This group should consist of a cross-functional selection of executives representing the organization's most important parts. The group should include members who support data governance as well as those who might be skeptical or less supportive of the concepts involved. The group should include influencers and thought leaders within the executive team. The Steering Committee should be headed by an Executive Sponsor who strongly supports data governance.

Data Governance Council

The Data Governance Council manages data governance initiatives. This group supports the development of data governance policies and metrics. They also support data governance by helping to resolve cross-functional issues, determine approaches to achieving strategies developed by the Steering Committee, and recommend funding prioritization. This team should be comprised of a cross-functional group of data practitioners.

Data Governance Office

The Data Governance Office provides an ongoing focus on enterprise-level data definitions and data management standards. This group coordinates roles for data stewards, data owners, and other roles. The group helps determine consistent processes by which enterprise standards are carried out. Depending on the size and scope of data governance activities within the organization, this group may act as a coordinating body, a project management team, or the only data governance team within the organization.

The Data Governance Office may also provide staff-supporting technologies utilized across the organization. These technologies may include:

- Data catalog
- Master data management
- Privacy and Access Technologies
- Data classification tools
- Data profiling and data quality tools

In this case, the Data Governance Office team helps to define the approach to utilizing these tools, supports users in implementing and configuring the tools, provides training, and may play a more active, hands-on role in managing and implementing content within the tools.

Data Stewardship Teams

Data Stewardship Teams are "Communities of interest focused on one or more specific subject-areas or projects, collaborating or consulting with project teams on data definitions and data management standards related to the focus. Consists of business and technical data stewards and data analysts."

Depending on the size and scope of given subject areas, the stewardship teams may consist of individuals or cross-functional teams. In some cases, the scope of an area might encompass many aspects or many related data sets. For example, a banking organization may require many teams to utilize data within the main transactional system, such as account management, trading, securities, currency management, etc. A healthcare organization may have multiple locations and the stewardship team managing location data will comprise operations experts, finance and accounting experts, facilities management teams, etc.

Reference

DAMA International. (2017). DAMA-DMBOK: Data Management Body of Knowledge. Second Edition. Technics Publications.

Other Roles

Other roles that may help implement successful data governance:

- **Executive Sponsor**: The main executive stakeholder who enthusiastically supports the aims of data governance. This executive should have experience in successfully shepherding data governance programs in similar organizations.

- **Stakeholders**: Anyone who works with data is automatically a stakeholder of the data governance program. Unfortunately, unless they know about data governance efforts within the organization, they may not be able to take advantage of the opportunities that result from these initiatives. Consistent, ongoing communication with stakeholders is a high priority for successful data governance.

- **Business Owners**: While organizations may define this role differently, the business owner is generally responsible for a specific set of data, usually defined by a software application or part of a software application. The business owner is usually the ultimate authority for determining the business requirements for a given application. He or she is responsible for making business decisions about the data set, including investment decisions. The business owner is also ultimately responsible for how data from that application is used across and outside the organization.

- **Technology Data Owners**: Again, this role's responsibilities may differ in various organizations, but usually, the technology data owner is responsible for ensuring the application and data achieve the business requirements determined by the business owner and their team. The technology owner works in tandem with the business owner to provide technology solutions to achieve business goals.

SMEs are probably the most important stakeholders in a data governance program.

- **Subject Matter Experts (SMEs)**: SMEs are probably the most important stakeholders in a data governance program. They may work within a business unit or a technology unit but have developed expertise in particular processes and data related to these processes. They are critical to the smooth functioning of their business unit's business and technical aspects. Due to this criticality, they are usually extremely busy and hard to get time with. Therefore, it is important to incorporate them into data governance activities in a thoughtful manner. Their knowledge is important to the success of data governance, so they should be encouraged to be part of the effort.

- **Project Managers/Implementation Leads**: As SMEs are important to understanding ongoing "Business as Usual" systems and processes, project managers and implementation leads are important to applying data governance to new projects. It's usually easier to apply new processes, such as data governance requirements, to new implementations, but care must be taken to ensure good communication regarding the prioritization and importance of data governance to new initiatives.

Implementations of new data sets are often on tight timelines. Agile project implementations focus first on minimum viable products and less on documentation. We must have enterprise acknowledgment that data governance is an imperative, not an add-on to implementations. If data governance activities such as creating definitions, following standards, implementing data quality and data observability reporting, etc., are included during implementations, less work will be required overall. Adding data governance after the fact will require more effort and may never be completed due to staff changes and a lack of executive interest.

CHAPTER 7

Data Quality

D ocumenting and improving data quality should be one of the main goals of a complete data governance program. Again, though, we may have many data quality issues across the data environment in a variety of data sets, in multiple databases and applications, and within data transformation and migration processes. Data quality issues can be seen across the organization. They may be hidden or they may be well known, creating workarounds that waste hours that could better be spent on value-added activities. How do we approach this embarrassment of riches?

Data quality issues may be as small as a misunderstanding regarding the meaning of a column. In one situation, data analysts assumed that a flag column meant that data for given clients could not be used for any processes beyond the client or aggregated into any summary results, internal or external. However, the flag was only set in the originating system to identify whether the client would receive marketing materials. Clarify this confusion with better data attribute descriptions or process descriptions during the transformation between the originating system and the analytical data mart.

Documenting and improving data quality should be one of the main goals of a complete data governance program.

Other data quality issues could be more significant, such as an acquired company or joint venture not collecting essential data elements to prove transactional information on common customers. This type of misinformation skews the information on basic business transactions, making results unreliable. Another situation I've seen includes basic sales metadata missing billing information. So, the client could be billed, but the proper organizational unit could not be identified to establish sales compensation rates. Making mistakes with the sales organization's compensation is a bad practice that makes for frustrated sales representatives.

This discussion will initially focus on data quality at the column or table level. As one might see by googling "Data Quality Dimensions," many aspects of data quality concerns exist. We will discuss other aspects of data quality elsewhere in this text.

Approach

I recommend following this data quality analysis approach:

1. Data profiling is used to understand the data at the column level.
2. Identify and document data quality standards pertaining to high-value or poor-quality data elements.
3. Measure conformance of actual data sets to data quality standards.
4. Apply data quality processes to improve conformance to data quality standards. This is obviously the most difficult and important data quality governance activity.
5. Monitor ongoing improvements or degradations in data quality conformance to standards.

Data Profiling

The initial step of data quality management should be profiling the data set. This allows us to understand what the data looks like. Even before working with subject matter experts and stakeholders to understand their issues with a data set, we should know what the data set contains. Conduct data profiling as soon as a data set is targeted for governance. This ensures that we can confirm the statements collected about the data from stakeholders. It's like taking your car to the shop. If the technician cannot recreate the problem, they cannot correct it. If we can't validate the issue in the data, we cannot improve data quality.

There are several excellent tools available in the marketplace to conduct profiling. These include traditional data processing tools, analytic toolsets, and data catalog tools. A few current examples include those available from Informatica, IBM Information Analyzer, Atlan, Talend Data Fabric, Toad Data Point, and Collibra. Data tools with purpose-built data profiling capabilities allow for the faster creation of interesting profile statistics and visualizations. But these tools can often have high costs. Additionally, licensing limitations may limit how you can deploy the resulting analytics across your organization. You could do basic profiling using structured query language (SQL) directly within a database. Depending on the size and accessibility of the data set, it can be queried directly from its source, pulled into another database or profiled from a flat file extract. Work with your data technology team to determine the best approach.

Profile analysis should include a basic review of the data set size, timeframe, and structure. Generally, we can think of data set sizes in ranges:

- **Small**: Less than 10,000 records
- **Medium**: Between 10,000 records up to a million records
- **Large**: over a million records.

If you have data sets reaching into the billions of records, you may want to identify ways to break them into smaller sets.

We should understand data sets in relation to the timeframe of the data involved. How old is this data? How has the data changed over time? As many companies have been in business for decades, they may have data sets that have aged and changed over time. While business and legal needs provide some purpose in keeping data over time, the meaning and content quality may change.

When profiling, dividing data sets into more recent and older categories may make sense. Often, older data will have lower compliance with current data standards. This will skew the analysis of data content. If you plan to integrate the data into an aggregated repository like a data warehouse or other analytical product, it may be appropriate to avoid very old data.

Next, we should understand the structure of the data set. Identify tables or entities and columns within each. If possible, for columns, document data types, and length, whether the columns are set as keys, not null, have other constraints or defaults set within the database or are part of indexes. This information can be read by profiling tools, data modeling tools, or by humans looking at the data definition language (DDL) that creates the tables in the database. If there are comments/descriptions or foreign-key relationships recorded within the database, bring this information into the analysis. Take note of the width (number of columns) of the data set. Wide tables of hundreds of columns will usually be more difficult to profile. They will usually make queries run longer. Consider analyzing wider tables in batches of fewer rows using time-based fields as filters.

Now, we can start actual profiling. Note the row count for each table. Use this to calculate percentages. We want to look at the data within each column, looking for the following:

For all data types:
- Nulls
    - Provides information for data quality completeness by column
    - Number of Null records/Number of not null records
    - Percent Null/Percent Not Null
- Minimum value/Maximum value
    - Provides the overall range of content for a column

For string or character-based columns:
- Minimum length (of not null values)/Maximum length

- o Provides data length for migration activities
- o May identify columns that are truncated when migrated

For numeric columns:
- Minimum/Maximum length:
  - o Decimal point
  - o Minimum/Maximum length before and after the decimal point
  - o Provides information for migration and potential data truncations

More sophisticated profiling:

- Unique values and counts: list the unique values in a column with record counts and percent of total for each value.
- Ranges of values: break the content into five (quintiles) or ten (deciles) groups from lowest to highest based on the unique value. Count how many records exist for each value.
- Outliers
  - o Look for values well outside the normal range within the data set.
  - o Example: Company Incorporation dates with a year of 905 are likely inaccurate
- Format, shape, or pattern(s) within the column.

- o For example, "nnnAAA" identifies a character set with six characters, starting with three numeric and ending with three alpha characters.
- o As an example, Social Security Numbers (SSNs) should have nine numeric characters or be formatted nnn-nn-nnnn. US Employer Identification Numbers (EINs) should have nine numeric characters or be formatted nn-nnnnnnn.
- o Number and percent of various formats or patterns within the column
- Relationships between content in multiple columns. Here again, data tools can do this type of analysis faster than writing the logic in SQL.

Data Quality Standards

This is the fun, people-focused part of data quality efforts. This exercise aims to identify Critical Data Elements (CDEs) and associated data standards for each. This asks the data owners, data stewards, and data governance teams to document what the data should be, ignoring for the moment what the data actually contains. Obviously, no data governance effort can create standards, measure, track, and improve data quality for every data element across the organization. Some sort of prioritization approach must be employed.

> *Documenting and improving data quality should be one of the main goals of a complete data governance program.*

Critical Data Elements

Many organizations use the concept of critical data elements (CDEs) to identify high-priority data elements for data quality improvement. I have spent hours in meetings discussing approaches to identifying CDEs. Don't get too bogged down in this effort. The idea is to identify those data columns with the most focus. Use critical data element designations to identify which data will require data standard definitions.

Some texts suggest that CDEs should be the elements required to perform important business functions or processes. When discussing this approach with a technical team, the question is which elements are NOT important for performing a function. "All our elements are important, or they wouldn't be in the system" is a fair answer. Unfortunately, no organization can afford the resources to monitor every element of a database or application to the Nth degree. Additionally, quality issues for important elements would be lost in the mass of data created.

One approach I've seen used successfully is identifying those data elements for a given subject that are required to provide a complete entity. This can be a strong approach for master data management. As an example, think of a contact record. The required elements for a complete personal contact record include:

- First Name
- Last Name
- Address Line 1
- City
- State
- Basic five-character Zip Code
- One phone number
- Email address.

Depending on the need, there might be others. For instance, employment records in the US require a Social Security Number. An employer might require an emergency contact name and phone number. Other master data subjects, like product, might require a set of critical data elements before the product can be considered complete: name, price, description, shipping cost, etc.

Don't confuse "required" in this instance with those fields required in each system managing this data. While the business managing a data set may see certain data elements as required for their work, the system creating the data may not enforce this requirement. The business team may expect this data to exist, the analysts using the data may assume it exists, but it may not for various technical or process-related reasons. If it does exist, it may not be of good quality. For example, data entry staff may enter poor-quality information just to pass a required field in the user interface.

Another approach to identifying CDEs is identifying data that requires attention for security, privacy, or other reasons. Dataversity published a helpful post in October 2023 noting:

The CDE philosophy can improve the organization's efficiency, security, and success. Examples of CDEs include customer data, protected health information, intellectual property, and financial information. A business's obligations or critical functions and processes can also qualify as a critical data element.

This approach would utilize the identification of PII, PHI, PCI, or other sensitive data elements in order to tag them as CDEs as well as with their sensitive data tags.

Other concerns noted by Dataversity in the above article include asking whether data elements are essential for running the business (certain security elements like user Id's and passwords), data elements with high costs, and the number of people, teams, and departments who are or might be using a data element.

Reference

Foote, Keith D. (2023, October 31). *Critical Data Elements Explained.* Dataversity.net. https://www.dataversity.net/critical-data-elements-explained/

One of my previous employers used a third approach to identifying CDEs. They first identified critical reports, which were those reports required by regulatory agencies, the board of directors, or other high-priority consumers. After identifying the critical reports, they tracked back the data elements used to create the reports into source systems and designated these as critical data elements. This process added an extra step, which required more time to complete but gave the data teams specific ways to identify critical data elements.

Data Standard Template

What should data standards include? As always, we want to document what is necessary without wasting effort on interesting, non-required information. According to data.gov, "a 'data standard' is a technical specification that describes how data should be stored or exchanged for the consistent collection and interoperability of that data across different systems, sources, and users." Data.gov also provides a starting list of data standards components that we can use to define our expectations related to data standards for individual data elements. These include data type, identifiers, vocabulary, schema, format, and API. You may want to add or remove content requirements when you create data standards for your organization.

Reference

Data.Gov Program Management Office in GSA TTS, The Office of Government and Information Services (OGIS), and the Office of Management and Budget (OMB). *Data Standards.* https://resources.data.gov/standards/concepts/

My recommendations for metadata for data standards include the following. This topic wraps into data catalog content, so you may also find that section helpful. As always, start small. It's better to document something and expand it later than to spend too much time in analysis paralysis.

Basic Demographics

- **Name**: Name the data standard to clearly identify the data element.
- **Business term**: Identify the commonly used business term associated with the data standard.
- **Term Definition**: Clearly define the business term. See the data dictionary section of this book for more details on creating good definitions.
- **Data Type**: Standard data type for this data like numeric, text, date, image, etc.
- **Identifiers**: Unique identifiers within your data governance system.

Content Specifications

- **Required/not required**: This may be required systematically or required to support a business process.
- **Vocabulary or ontology**: If a specific industry or organizational vocabulary set or ontology defines the options for content within this element, identify the ontology.
- **Sensitivity Type**: If the element is part of an identified set of sensitive data elements like PII or PHI, identify such.

Location

- Technical or physical name of the element (column or field name).
- Identify the database or application location of the data element. For instance, a database column can be located from [Database].[Schema].[Table].[Column] specifications. Additional information, such as screen and field location identification, might be useful in reference to application user interfaces.

Lineage (These items may be more difficult to identify, but if you have a subject matter expert available, you can gather the basics.)

- Where appropriate, identify the input format in which the data is initially created. For example, a given element might be filled via the originating user interface via free text, require a numeric value, be selected using a list-based dropdown, be created by system calculation, be set via state-based trigger, or have other system-based requirements.
- Originating systems and business processes.
- Modifying systems and business processes.
- Consuming systems and business processes.

Ownership and Usage

- Business owner or manager responsible for the organizational unit that creates, manages, stores, maintains, and deletes the given data element. Identifying and obtaining ownership acceptance of data can be one of the most challenging parts of data governance.
- Data steward: if your organization intends to identify data stewards for specific data elements, note those.
- Subject matter expert: it can be helpful to data consumers to know who can answer questions about specific data elements.
- Access methods, technical specifications, etc., that can be used by system or analyst consumers to utilize the data element.

Data Quality Dimensions

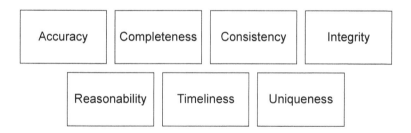

While many organizations, data vendors, and educational sites have somewhat different lists of data quality dimensions, we should cover these here to set the stage for discussion. DAMA-

DMBOK lists the following data quality dimensions. I've broken up the definitions into paragraphs to support further discussion. The National Park Service has an excellent chart of data quality dimensions with helpful examples in their domain. I've noted them below.

Accuracy: Accuracy refers to the degree to which data correctly represents 'real-life' entities. Accuracy is difficult to measure unless an organization can reproduce data collection or manually confirm the accuracy of records.

Most measures of accuracy rely on comparison to a data source that has been verified as accurate, such as a system of record or data from a reliable source (e.g., Dun and Bradstreet Reference Data and Wall Street Journal Currency Rates). (DAMA-DMBOK)

NPS example: The home telephone number for a customer's record does not match the actual telephone number. (noted as Accurate compared to reality).

NPS example: An applicant's income reported on the application form does not match what is in the database. (noted as accurate vs. surrogate source)

Completeness: Completeness refers to whether all required data is present. Completeness can be measured at the data set, record, or column level.

Does the data set contain all the records expected? Are records populated correctly? (Records with different states or statuses may have different expectations for completeness.)

Are columns/attributes populated to the level expected? Some columns are mandatory. Optional columns are populated only under specific conditions.

Assign completeness rules to a data set with varying levels of constraint: Mandatory attributes that require a value, data elements with conditional and optional values, and inapplicable attribute values. Data set level measurements may require comparison to a source of record or may be based on historical population levels. (DAMA-DMBOK)

NPS Example: An indicator for a spouse is set to "yes," but spousal data is not present.

Consistency: Consistency can refer to ensuring that data values are consistently represented within a data set and between data sets, and consistently associated across data sets. It can also refer to the size and composition of data sets between systems or across time.

Consistency may be defined between one set of attribute values and another attribute set within the same record (record-level consistency), between one set of attribute values and another attribute set in different records (cross-record consistency), or between one set of attribute values and the same attribute set with the same record at different points in time (temporal consistency).

Encapsulate consistency constraints as a set of rules that specify consistent relationships between values of attributes, either across a record or message or along all values of a single attribute (such as a range or list of valid values). For example, one might expect that the number of transactions each day does not exceed 105% of the running average number of transactions for the previous 30 days.

NPS Example: The same applicant is present in two databases or systems and has a different name, address, or dependents.

Integrity: Data Integrity (or Coherence) includes ideas associated with completeness, accuracy, and consistency. In data, integrity usually refers to either referential integrity (consistency between data objects via a reference key contained in both objects) or internal consistency within a data set such that there are no holes or missing parts.

Data sets without integrity are seen as corrupted or have data loss. Data sets without referential integrity have 'orphans' (invalid reference keys) or 'duplicates' (identical rows, which may negatively affect aggregation functions).

Measure the level of orphan records as a raw count or a percentage of the data set (DAMA-DMBOK).

NPS Example: The summary of accounts for a given district does not contain valid entries for the district.

Reasonability: Reasonability asks whether a data pattern meets expectations. For example, does a distribution of sales across a geographic area make sense based on what we know about the customers in that area? Measurements of reasonability can take different forms. For example, base reasonability compared to benchmark data or past instances of a similar data set (e.g., sales from the previous quarter).

Some ideas about reasonability may be perceived as subjective. If this is the case, work with data consumers to articulate the basis of their expectations of data to formulate objective comparisons. After establishing benchmark measurements of reasonability, you can objectively compare new instances of the same data set to detect change.

Timeliness: The concept of data timeliness refers to several characteristics of data. Understand measures of timeliness in terms of expected volatility—how frequently data is likely to change and for what reasons.

Data currency measures whether data values are the most up-to-date version of the information. Relatively static data, such as reference data values like country codes, may remain current for a long time. Volatile data remains current for only a short time.

Another time of timeliness, latency, measures the time between when the data was created and when it was made available for use (DAMA-DMBOK). This measure of timeliness can be important when data is moved repeatedly between systems, like loading transactional data into a data repository.

A change of address is needed to schedule an inspection, but it is not available to the field office, and the inspector leaves without the proper data.

On Monday, an applicant's change of address is updated in the Applicant record or origin file. Still, the record is propagated to the main Program database after the weekend cycle (Friday night). That record has a concurrency float of five days between the record-of-origin file and the record-of-reference database (noted as Concurrency Data Quality Dimension).

Uniqueness: Uniqueness states that no entity exists more than once within the data set. Asserting the uniqueness of the entities within a data set implies that a key value relates to each unique entity, and only that specific entity, within the data set. Measure uniqueness by testing against key structures (DAMA-DMBOK).

NPS Example: One applicant has multiple applicant records (evident when an applicant gets duplicate, even conflicting, notices.)

Validity: Validity refers to whether data values are consistent with a defined domain of values. A domain of values may be a defined set of valid values (such as a reference table), a range of values, or a value that can be determined via rules. The data type, format, and precision of expected values must be accounted for when defining the domain. Data may also only be valid for a specific length of time, for example, RFID (radio frequency ID) or some scientific data sets. Validate data by comparing it to domain constraints. Remember that data may be valid (i.e., it may meet domain requirements) and still not be accurate or correctly associated with particular records. (DAMA – DMBOK)

NPS Example: A US address has a state abbreviation that is not valid (not in the valid state abbreviation list).

NPS Example: A property address shows a Michigan Zip Code but a Florida city and state (noted as Relationship Validity).

Regardless of the exact Data Quality Dimensions, definitions, and associated examples, these definitions provide ways to think about data quality issues. Your mileage will vary. Don't spend a lot of time deciding which dimension your issue fits. The important idea is that data quality is much more than counting the number of Null values in a given column in today's data load. The point is to look at data in ways that allow us to measure conformance to expectations, identify issues, track root causes, correct problems, and measure progress toward improving data quality.

Please also note that the above Data Quality Dimensions reach across different levels of data structures. For example, completeness might refer to the completeness of the data values in a specific column in a table, like a descriptive attribute within a master data table. Or completeness might refer to the completeness of a daily data load. Timeliness often refers to the timeliness of data loads or refreshes of data related to when the data was originally collected or most recently modified, as in the NPS examples. In this section of this text, I'll focus on data quality dimensions reflective of columnar data quality. In other sections, like Data Observability, I will discuss data quality dimensions focused on the full set of data and processing thereof.

Reference

DAMA International. (2017). DAMA-DMBOK: Data Management Body of Knowledge. Second Edition. Technics Publications.

United States Department of the Interior. Office of the Chief Information Officer. (2008, August). Data Quality Management Guide. www.nps.gov. https://www.nps.gov/gis/egim/library/DataQuality_2008_0824_DOI%20Data%20Quality%20Management%20Guide.pdf

Data Quality Rules

The next level of data standards we need to cover is data quality rules. Here, we dive more deeply into the specifications of the data element. These specifications relate to the data requirements used to create the data in the originating system. Still, more importantly, they should define the user and reporting expectations related to data quality. Data quality rules are used in automated and reporting systems that perform testing for data quality anomalies.

Many books are available on data quality rules, data quality evaluation, and automation. Additionally, there are various philosophies about creating data quality rules within an organization. We once again realize we cannot possibly tackle every potential problem in our data environment. In addition to focusing on the critical data elements (CDEs), we cannot possibly test for every potential problem with individual CDEs.

Let's discuss ways to identify the most important issues for our CDEs. This is where we need to involve our stakeholders: data consumers who should be able to communicate their expectations, data owners who can discuss existing system requirements or processes, and subject matter experts who can discuss the historic and current data quality issues and challenges.

While products are coming into the broader data marketplace that can utilize artificial intelligence and machine learning (AI/ML) to detect data quality issues, they may not detect the issues you want to identify. For instance, AI/ML data quality monitors can detect anomalies in data like outliers, which are those values that lay well outside the standard expectations for the data element, or find changes from historical patterns, which may not assume that the historic data was good quality. These products have their use but do not entirely substitute for human knowledge of the context and expectations for data.

Take, for instance, recent findings of data anomalies in the Social Security Administration (SSA), which seem to indicate that recipients are over 150 years old. However, staff at SSA were aware of the poor data quality and used other controls as workarounds. AI/ML couldn't detect those.

Data quality rules define the details of what subject matter experts expect from data to support requirements for both original processing of transactional and master data, but also secondary usage for analytics, data sharing, and other purposes. In "Automating Data Quality Monitoring," Stanley and Schwartz state that

Rules allow an SME to express a requirement for a given dataset based on their knowledge of the system that generated the data or the business context in which the data was collected. An SME can write a rule saying a column should never be NULL in the data's past, present, or future.

Data quality rules enable us to define the specific logic required to test whether data matches the standards that SMEs and users expect of the data. These rules may start with simple logic but may be more complex to create than initially expected. For instance, I have seen logic required to calculate simple completeness metrics run into fairly lengthy queries with 4-5 tables involved and including multiple filters to identify the correct state of given master data entities (i.e., active versus obsolete) and including appropriate descriptive dimensions for reporting (i.e., which business entity references the entity). However, the underlying rule can still be written in clear business language for inclusion in the data standard and data catalog.

Reference

Stanley, Jeremy; Schwartz, Paige. Automating Data Quality Monitoring (p. 59). O'Reilly Media. Kindle Edition.

In Chapter 6 of "Practical Data Quality," Robert Hawker provides a framework for writing "a clearly understandable business definition of a rule, which can then be converted into a programmatic check of data with a data quality tool." Hawker walks through various considerations for data quality rules, including:

- **Rule Scope:** This provides the "where" clause of the queries used to test the rule. Hawker uses an example of a rule applicable to the "Services" category of suppliers, which must include a VAT number. We may not immediately know the specifics of the data quality rule scope, but can discover this during the analysis and testing of the rule.

- **Rule Weightings:** These are used to allow prioritization of certain rules and minimization of the impact of others.

- **Rule Dimensions:** Hawker describes rule dimensions as a method for grouping data quality rules, especially if a data product has been assigned many rules across different data quality dimensions.

- **Rule Priorities:** These are used to provide analysts and data practitioners with the ability to focus on the highest priority rules. I'd recommend creating the highest priority rules first, then working to improve these measures.

- **Rule Thresholds:** These provide targets or goals to which data quality efforts should aspire. Hawker identifies Thresholds as the most important aspect of creating data quality rules. I agree. While we can review data quality conformance to expectations and trend changes in quality over time, it's very difficult to see whether we are achieving expected results without a target. But a target threshold gives the data team a more achievable focus than just trending results over time.

Reference

Hawker, Robert. (2023). *Practical Data Quality.* Packt Publishing.

Data Quality Rule Content

How do you write data quality rules? When a team sits down to document rules, getting started and knowing what sort of information to include can be daunting. Arkady Maydanchik provides excellent suggestions on DataQualityPro.com.

He first lists five categories of data quality rules:

1. **Attribute domain constraints** restrict the allowed values of individual data attributes. They are the most basic of all data quality rules.

2. **Relational integrity rules** are derived from the relational data models and enforce the identity and referential integrity of the data.

3. **Rules for historical data** include timeline constraints and value patterns for time-dependent value stacks and event histories.

4. **Rules for state-dependent objects** constrain the lifecycle of objects described by so-called state-transition models.

5. **General dependency rules** describe complex attribute relationships, including constraints on redundant, derived, partially dependent, and correlated attributes.

Attribute Domain Constraints

Attribute domain constraints can be the most intuitive place to start. As Maydanchik notes, some requirements for attributes may be discernable by reviewing the data model. However, we should include Subject Matter Experts (SMEs) from both source and consuming systems in discussions about attribute data quality. For example, a database or source system application user interface may not require that a particular attribute have content. Still, the data element may be required for reporting or incorporation into a complete product description.

Some attribute-level data issues I've seen over time include:

- Missing values or completeness for attributes required for reporting.

- Inadequate content; i.e., there should be more information in the data attribute than there is.

- Default values used inappropriately where users either forgot to change the default or skipped the field.

- False values are used to fill required fields. Often, data entry is slowed by required fields in the user interface, so staff creates ways to skip required fields by entering short words or punctuation instead of meaningful values.

- Poor quality content, such as incomplete street address information.

- Poorly formatted data that doesn't conform to the expected shape, like phone numbers and identifiers. For example, Social Security Numbers and employer identifiers in the US should be nine digits (nnn-nn-nnnn or nn-nnnnnnn).

- Formatting and incorrect transformations of dates and timestamps. When data moves between systems, dates and timestamps may not transform correctly into accurate information.

- Appropriate range of content. For example, birth dates should be expected within a manageable range of time, not back into the ninth century.

- Null values versus blank entries, leading or trailing zeros, and spaces.

- Special characters that may not be handled well during data movements. For example, even commas may cause issues when automation mistakes them for field separators.

- Truncation of long fields when data moves between systems. This often occurs in text fields, but pay attention to decimal cutoffs in numeric fields as well.

Relational Integrity Constraints

Once we've reviewed potential data quality rules focused on specific attributes or data columns, we can go on to more complex rules. Since we focus on getting data governance projects and programs moving forward, we won't get into deep detail on complex data quality. Some examples of relationship-based data quality issues include:

- Orphaned records caused by missing dimensional records, like missing customer records for transactions.

- Transactional records 'stubbed' to non-meaningful dimensional records. For example, locations tagged to "N/A" or "TBD".

- Duplicate records that may match the referring record. An example might be a patient with multiple records matching an account reference.

Reference

Maydanchik, Arkady. *Data Quality Rules Tutorial 1 of 4: Attribute Domain Constraints.* www.dataqualitypro.com.
https://www.dataqualitypro.com/blog/data-quality-rules-attribute-domain-constraints-arkady-maydanchik

Historical Data Quality Rules

Data changes over time both in quality and purposefully to track changes in the underlying information being described in the data. The data governance team may want to focus more on the quality of more recent data and improve data quality moving forward. Analysis of the historic data may be less of a priority in early implementations of data governance.

Reference

Maydanchik, Arkady. *Data Quality Rule Tutorial 3 of 4: Rules for Historical Data.* www.dataqualitypro.com.
https://www.dataqualitypro.com/blog/historical-data-quality-rules

Event History Data Quality Rules

In the fourth of Maydanchik's blog postings on dataqualitypro.com, he describes proposed event history data quality rules. Much of an organization's data focuses on events, whether those are transactional events (i.e., sales, orders, patient visit, lab accession, investment, etc.), changes within a master data domain (i.e., address change, change of marriage status, price increase, etc.), or some other event reflected in the data set.

Reference

Maydanchik, Arkady. *Data Quality Rule Tutorial 4 of 4: Rules for Event Histories.* www.dataqualitypro.com.
https://www.dataqualitypro.com/blog/event-histories-data-quality-rules

Data Quality Rule Implementation

We've explored some areas where we want to create data quality rules. The next step is to create logic and implement the rules in a tool to test the data. Use several toolsets to run data quality testing, including creating basic SQL code or utilizing some of the popular reporting tools like Power BI, Tableau, and QlikView. There are more expensive toolsets with more functionality, like Informatica Cloud Data Quality and Collibra's Data Quality toolset. I recommend starting slowly with some basic tests and building out a library of tests as they are reviewed and validated by subject matter experts, users, and analysts.

Data Quality Improvement

Here, we get into the challenging territory of working with business and technical staff to improve data quality. This can be the most challenging aspect of data governance activities. It requires patience and perseverance, knowledge of the subject area and the business, facilitation, and flexibility in working with stakeholders across the organization. Therefore, data stewards and SMEs can help here. Some issues may be fairly easy to resolve. Some may require a significant investment of time and financial resources. Some, unfortunately, may not be resolved in the near term.

Generally, data cleansing is not a best practice for correcting data quality issues.

To understand the process to make data quality improvements, conduct root cause analysis. Generally, data cleansing is not a best practice for correcting data quality issues. Eventually, once data quality issues have been resolved or corrected at the source, some data cleansing may need to be performed within affected systems. However, if data is cleansed as it is moved between systems, say, a transactional system and a data repository, the data quality will never improve. The owners of the original system will not be aware of problems within their systems. They will not make changes that consumers need to prove quality information from the source. Additionally, over time, data cleansing efforts will continue to grow and migrate across the organization. Not all users will cleanse the data the same way, creating different results for different uses. This just exacerbates the situation.

Once potential resolutions are identified, they will need to be evaluated for potential implementation. Some will be relatively easy to implement at the source, such as adding a value to a drop-down list, requiring further user training, or updating existing master data records. Other resolutions may be much more complex, say performing a widespread analysis to identify and remove records relating to expired systems across a large organization. DataQualityPro.com recommends identifying data quality issues and resolution impacts in terms of frequency but also in terms of cost and time spent and reduction. As this blog notes, the most frequently found issues may not have the biggest impact on cost.

Monitoring Data Quality Improvements

We need to monitor results once we have implemented changes to impact data quality. Many organizations fail to monitor the results of initiatives across the board. It's hard to support additional changes if we cannot measure the results of improvements. Since we have implemented reporting to profile data quality, this system can be leveraged to report on changes to data quality over time. Note that this must include the ability to track trending of data quality issues. This may require the storage of data quality metrics periodically or the utilization of toolsets that can allow these snapshots.

Note that changes to data quality may appear in the results as "data scars" or "data shocks." In "Automating Data Quality Monitoring", Stanley and Schwartz describe data scars as "a period of time for a given set of data where a subset of records are invalid or anomalous and cannot be trusted by any systems operating on those records in the future." Even repairing data scars may affect data used downstream in AI/ML models or analysis.

In Chapter 7 of "Practical Data Quality," Robert Hawker provides guidance on implementing data quality reporting. He recommends three levels of reporting:

- **High-level data quality dashboards:** to allow senior stakeholders and data owners to monitor quality.

- **Detailed data quality reporting/Rule results reporting:** to allow data stewards to review rules and identify targets for data remediation efforts.

- **Failed Data Reporting:** for data producers to use as a list of records that need to be corrected.

This portfolio of reporting can, of course, be augmented by other reporting as your organization sees fit. Additionally, new toolsets are coming online that utilize AI/ML technology to identify changes in data over time. This methodology presupposes that existing data is of acceptable quality and that changes should be investigated and challenged. But, combined with rules-based analysis, this could provide valuable insight.

Reference

Hawker, Robert. (2023). *Practical Data Quality*. Packt Publishing.

Evaluate Results and Select Additional Data Quality Targets

The final step in a data quality journey is to review the results of your efforts and go back around to find further targets for improvement. As in other systems-based processes, the success or lack of success of initial efforts will either point out that changes have not created expected improvements, identify new targets for change, or, unfortunately, determine that the changes have created new issues. The process of data quality improvement is a never-ending cycle. It's not a one-and-done project where we can declare victory and go home. There are always new data sets to improve, old ones to improve or replace, and interesting new ways to combine data. Data quality can be extremely frustrating but often very rewarding.

Reference

Hawker, Robert. (2023). *Practical Data Quality*. Packt Publishing.

Moses, B., Gavish, L. and Vorwerck, M. (2022). *Data Quality Fundamentals.* O'Reilly Media, Inc.

Stanley, J. and Schwartz, Paige. (2024). *Automating Data Quality Monitoring.* O'Reilly Media, Inc.

Southekal, P. (2023) *Data Quality.* Wiley.

Jones, Andrew. (2023). *Driving Data Quality with Data Contracts.* Packt Publishing.

CHAPTER 8

Data Stewardship

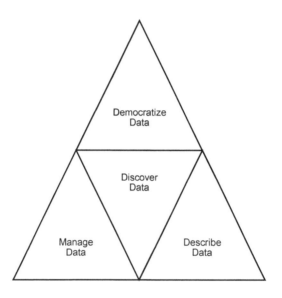

Data stewardship is the people part of data governance, and perhaps the most important aspect of governing data. The data governance community has different views on what a data steward is and their responsibilities. In my experience, data stewards are responsible for working directly with organizational data and stakeholders. Data stewards are usually Subject Matter Experts (SMEs) who have in-depth knowledge of the business area, the data, and the related processes. These staff members can understand and work with businesspeople, technologists, other team members, and the data governance team to understand the needs of all constituencies, identify problems, work through complex situations, and 'steward' solutions. This role requires patience and persistence, as well as business and technical knowledge of the data and systems involved. The role can be frustrating for a variety of reasons, including a lack of organizational support for change, the need to balance competing demands, the sheer amount of work required, and a lack of understanding by siloed teams. The data steward must be a 'people person,' with a strategic understanding of the situations and underlying technologies and constraints. Often, the data steward will either have spent years within the organization learning these skills and the history of the data or have worked in a similar role in another organization. The data steward can often be the most valuable member of the data governance organization.

Data Stewards may be identified and assigned to data areas in various approaches. I like Seiner's description in Chapters 7 and 8 of Non-Invasive Data Governance. Here, he describes three types of data stewards: the Operational Data Steward, the Domain Data Steward, and the Data Steward Coordinator. The Operational Data Steward is a person who has, as part of their role, an inherent "relationship to data."

"But I do say that each person who defines, produces, and uses data in your organization has a certain level of accountability or responsibility for how data are defined, produced, and used."

We often see a SME within a business unit who has become the expert in a system or a set of systems. This person is the "go to" expert who everyone asks questions about that data set. They may be a businessperson who has been in the unit for years, an analyst who has been working with the data across multiple roles, or a technical resource who has been building interfaces from that data during many projects. This person can be a good candidate for a named Operational Steward.

The Domain Data Steward may be a more intentional role identified by and reporting, at least a dotted line, to the data governance team. This person usually supports data related to a specific subject area. In organizations I've worked with, I focused on products or services, types of customers, or other mastered or dimensional-type data. However, domain stewards might also be identified and assigned to subject areas representing processes within the business. For example, a business unit specializing in certain types of business and customers has processes like fulfillment, operations, orders-to-cash, revenue, accounting, etc. Seiner notes that if the team is large enough, an organization may require a Data Steward Coordinator. This person will help identify, organize, facilitate, train, guide, and perhaps measure the team of Operational and Domain data stewards. This role may be located within the centralized data governance team.

Reference

Seiner, Robert S. (2014). Non-Invasive Data Governance: The Path of Least Resistance and Greatest Success. Technics Publications.

In "Data Stewardship in Action," Pui Shing Lee identifies four main pillars of Data Stewardship: Discover Data, Describe Data, Manage Data, and Democratize Data.

Discover Data

Lee describes data discovery as identifying the "end-to-end data estate through connected data." This documentation would consist of listing the high-level data systems and data sets and identifying the process, or lineage, of data flows between data sets. Data discovery may range from the higher level down to the attribute level data flows, which describe the intricate extraction, transformation, and loading processes that move data into, within, and outside an organization. In our initial overview of the data environment within the organization, we can start with a high-level inventory of data systems, data sets, and data flows. A more detailed evaluation of data lineage can wait for data governance project work.

What does "discovering data" look like for the data steward? This hands-on activity requires the data steward to analyze the data set, work with the team or teams who create the data, and learn how data moves across the organization. This requires the ability to query or profile the data to understand content both across (columns within given tables or files) and down (what content exists at the row level in the data). So, what structures exist in the data and what content exists within those structures? Questions the steward might want to ask and document:

- What are the tables/files and columns/fields within the data set?
- How many rows exist in the data set? How often are they updated?
- How many new records are recorded in a time period?
- What is the profile of the data (recall Data Profiling in Chapter 3)?
- Who is responsible for creating, managing, updating, archiving, and delivering this data?
- Where is this data used beyond the originating system? Who is responsible for target systems?
- Is this data modified during any data flows within the organization?
- Refer back to the Data Quality chapter for details on data profiling.

Describe Data

Here, Lee recommends describing data "through applied business context … and how it can be used to inform decision-making."

For example, a data steward might analyze customer data to understand customer preferences and behavior, which can then be used to inform marketing and product development decisions.

Our process of inventorying major data sets, risks, value propositions, and data governance functional needs provides a framework by which to describe data. This inventory can be used as described to create a roadmap for data governance projects, but it will also be instrumental for many other data projects across the organization. For instance, architecture projects such as prioritizing system upgrades, identifying risks for penetration testing, and documenting process flows for regulatory compliance can be based on this inventory. The data catalog can document the above information (recall the data catalog discussion from Chapter 9).

Manage Data

Here, Lee identifies processes needed for testing and monitoring data quality, validating data, and cleansing data. We might add monitoring data processes with observability reporting, managing master data for consistency and completeness, documenting new data processes added to the environment, precisely removing data processes that are no longer required, listing new data coming into the organization, and validating data shared externally from the organization.

We include processes where the data steward works with a team of relevant stakeholders to identify issues within the data set and works with the team, business owners, and IT staff to resolve issues. I've worked with new data stewards who've identified hundreds of data issues within their data subject. These ranged from missing values within a dropdown list to missing processes, like processes required to close out locations. I've also worked with teams who found data issues to be so intractable that they hadn't been resolved in many years. Data stewardship can be a long, frustrating process.

Democratizing Data

According to a helpful article from DataCamp.org, data democratization "is the process of making data more accessible to a wider range of people within the organization or society." Data democratization requires elevating data from its silo-based organizational constraints and enabling its use across the organization. According to DataCamp, this involves not only allowing people to access the data but also providing "tools and skills that they need to analyze and interpret data effectively."

The data steward plays an important role in democratizing data by supporting all the efforts of data governance, modeling ways of using data to facilitate data-driven decision-making, data sharing across the organization, and teaching cross-functional teams about specific data sets.

Lee notes that democratizing data is the most difficult aspect of data stewardship. This can be true for many reasons. Lee points out that resistance to change can be a factor in the inability to democratize data across the enterprise. Resistance to data governance and data stewardship may be due to the implementation of data policies across the enterprise. Some of this resistance may be due to details within the data set, the software, the business cases, etc. Some may be due to a lack of experience or interest in coordinating policies with other teams. Lee includes these aspects of data stewardship as part of the democratization of data.

Frequently, data implementations tend to be built within business and IT siloes. Projects are imagined, funded, built, maintained, and implemented within localized teams in the organization. People focus on completing their work and achieving results for given projects and periods. Without imaginative data leadership, teams often ignore or forget the possibilities of sharing data with other teams or utilizing high-quality data created by other parts of the organization. Sometimes, this occurs due to organizational politics, which encourage departmental appropriation and control of data sets. This book will not attempt to recommend solutions for these challenges, but it is important to know that they may occur in many organizations.

Reference

Lee, Pui Shing. (2024). *Data Stewardship in Action.* Packt Publishing.

Data Camp (July 22, 2024). *What is Data Democratization? Unlocking the Power of Data Cultures for Business Use.*
https://www.datacamp.com/blog/what-does-democratizing-data-mean.

CHAPTER 9

Data Catalog

D ocumenting and providing metadata to users can solve many organizational issues around data. Simply providing analysts, data scientists, and report developers with a data dictionary of your organization's most important data systems can go a long way toward enhancing data use across the organization.

In my experience, the data dictionary is second in popularity to the business glossary and acronym list within a data catalog. The business glossary and acronym list provides the key to helping businesspeople and analysts understand how the business is managed. The relationships in the data catalog between business terms/acronyms and technical metadata in the data dictionary allow users to translate the business language to the data used across the organization to run the business. Database technologies are designed to perform a job and are implemented to perform their specific processes in the most efficient manner possible.

Database naming conventions, structures, processes, and storage are not intended to support analytics or provide data easily to other systems. Thus, we have created a situation where businesspeople and technical professionals need to be able to understand the same data in different ways. This is one of the main purposes of a data catalog.

Business glossary: Provides business users like managers, new hires, analysts, data scientists, etc., with the ability to understand the meaning of words and abbreviations used across the organization. Includes:

- List of business terms with definitions.
- List of acronyms and related business terms along with their definitions.

The business glossary allows the data governance team and Subject Matter Experts to relate business language with technical language by creating relationships in the data catalog between technical metadata and content in the business glossary.

Data catalog: The entirety of the system that provides users information about metadata, data about data, across all aspects and many applications within the organization. This metadata may include technical database metadata, business metadata describing the data in business terms, process metadata about how the data is and can be used, lineage metadata about how data moves between systems, etc.

Data dictionary: The portion of the data catalog that focuses on technical metadata describing database structures within the organization. Specifically, this includes the physical database models, including databases, schemas, tables, columns, etc., plus attributes further describing these structural components. The data dictionary may also include relationships between data structures, like foreign key relationships. We can present it in diagram form as a relational data model or as a list showing tables, columns, data types, keys, descriptions, etc. There may also be other forms of models, such as subject area models or logical models.

As with other aspects of data governance, the data catalog may be implemented in various ways on various platforms. An organization may start small using simple tools like Excel to gather and organize both a business glossary and a data dictionary. Over time, more sophisticated tools may be required along with better ways to share the information across stakeholder groups in the organization. We can accomplish this by posting the glossary and dictionary over an intranet or incorporating some of the open source data dictionary tools. With the ability of funding to invest in industry-leading tools, an organization may want to investigate tools like Collibra, Informatica's Cloud toolset, Atlan, and others.

Beware that developing the data catalog is much more work-intensive than simply purchasing a metadata platform.

Regardless of the automation capabilities of the more sophisticated metadata platforms, significant effort is required to gather, organize, plan, input, and manage metadata, especially business information. These platforms can be very helpful, but like any system, must be carefully managed and curated to provide maximum value to users. Metadata management is as much a living process as any other part of data governance. As with other work described in this book, start small and build over time.

Business Glossary	Data Dictionary	Governance Metadata	Process Metadata
• Acronyms • Business Terms • Definitions	• Technical Metadata • Reference Data • System Inventory	• Data Standards • Data Quality Rules • Roles and Responsibilities	• Data Flow Lineage • Data Observability

Business Metadata

Business metadata within the data catalog is what we use to document a shared language between business team members, cross-departmental project teams, and technical teams. While many departments work in silos of information using their own vocabularies of operations, finance, sales, technologies, or industry languages, it helps to have a place where people can go to understand how to use various words, phrases, and abbreviations within the organization. Even within the same organization, words like customer, patient, and client may be used differently depending on context. If an attempt is made to document such vocabulary, it can help facilitate communication between teams. Most projects in modern organizations require cross-functional cooperation that a good business glossary can facilitate.

Most organizations have a list of acronyms and business terms shared informally or provided to new hires upon onboarding. A frustrated intern may have started this list many years back, added to it over time, or never curated. I once started a position where, within a year, I gathered almost 900 specific business terms and acronyms from across the organization, just by collecting them informally from other lists I encountered. In another position, I gathered over 3,000 as part of my position in data governance. These terms included company-specific words like "Legal Entity" that were used differently than in a legal sense. They used it to refer to a company site or location. The terms included industry-specific terms or abbreviations, such as CUSIP or BCBS239.

The process of cataloging data tables and columns, reports, files, and fields will provide a structured process by which to collect business terms and acronyms of meaning to Stakeholders. One way to start is to review applicable data structures, like tables and columns. For example, there is likely to be one or more business terms describing the data in a table. The same applies to each column.

Although there are likely to be many "system" tables and columns, such as keys between tables and audit columns (tracking create and update timestamps, source systems, and users), pay attention to the tables and columns describing business information: the who, what, when, how, where, and why of the business. Document these, talk to stakeholders, understand how the business talks about this information, and write it down. This becomes the basis for the business glossary. Review reporting with an eye to how business-side stakeholders receive their information. This is where your embedded analysts come in handy, those people who work within business units, operational units, sales units, marketing, finance, etc., who know the language of management and executives and can translate that into data-focused meaning.

When creating the business glossary, you want to collect and document several types of metadata:

- **Business terms**: The words used by people across the organization to describe people, places, things, activities, dates, times, processes, etc. At this phase, don't worry too much about multiple terms that may refer to the same concept or be used differently within various stakeholder groups. This situation tends to send panic through the team, but it can also be documented if approached calmly and methodically. Don't strive for perfection. Strive for improvement.

- **Acronyms**: My favorite acronym is TLA (Three-Letter Acronym). Every industry has a plethora of acronyms. Every organization thinks they have more than everyone else. Many organizations use the same TLAs for multiple terms and there may even be multiple TLAs that essentially mean the same thing. This can be particularly prevalent on the technology side when systems are rebranded or vendors change names and veterans continue to refer to a technology by the name they used when first encountering the tool. We still "dial" our phones, right?

- **Definitions:** Don't forget the definitions when collecting business terms and acronyms. It's nice to know the term the TLA refers to, but you must also know its definition. Users need to understand what a term means and what the acronym means.

- **People Roles**: While building a business glossary, it can be helpful to identify the people related to this information. This may include Subject Matter Experts (SMEs) who are knowledgeable about the term or business related to the term. It may include catalog ownership of the term and any curation responsibilities. It may include a Data Steward or other responsible analyst.

- **Priority**: At some point in your journey, you will want to identify Critical Data Elements (CDEs). This is particularly important for focusing governance efforts on data quality monitoring and quality improvement efforts. Some industries also use CDEs to identify those data elements to trace through all data process flows for external or regulatory reporting. Identifying business terms with their CDE status can help in this process.

- **Business term attributes:** Once we have the beginning of a business glossary, we can add other metadata to business terms that might be useful for the organization. Some information I've seen added includes:

  o **Domain**: Subject area of the business term/acronym identifying what information this term relates to. For example, client, patient, location, legal entity, finance, etc.

  o **Synonyms**: Many terms used in business might mean the same thing. For example, I've seen Test, Test Code, and others used interchangeably.

  o **Terms with Multiple Meanings**: There may come a time when it is not possible to obtain agreement on the meaning of a particular term. In that case, it may be necessary to document the definition of the term in multiple ways. Be sure to identify why and who uses each definition.

  o **Hierarchies of Terms**: Terms might relate in a variety of ways. For example, we can organize the sales organization in a way that relates to Regions, States, and Countries. That hierarchy might be created with cross-term references.

  o **Related Terms**: Terms might be like other terms, and thus, the organization might want to group them together and show how the terms in the group are related. For example, we might identify Tax Identifiers for employees, contractors, vendors, or clients. While a Tax Identifier may be a Social Security Number for employees or contractors, it might be an Employer Identification Number for vendors, clients, and other organizations.

- **Association to Data Sets and Attributes:** Here is where we start to integrate business language with technical data. We want to identify which specific data sets and attributes relate to the business terms we are defining. In some cases, this can be fairly easy, like identifying Patient Name or Account Number. In other cases, database structures may be less easy to define and, therefore, more difficult to link to business terms.

Facilitate this process with some of the newer AI-supported data tools. Still, it must be reviewed and validated by humans who understand the underlying data. As we know, not all data content reflects the names of the columns or fields where it is stored. Additionally, there may be nuances created by system change over time that might not be reflected in naming conventions. An additional consideration is that some business terms used in the organization and documented in the glossary may not refer to specific data elements like column or field names. These terms are helpful to document to create a shared understanding of organizational language, but they don't necessarily connect directly to any specific piece of data. The business glossary is a good place to store these definitions.

- **Data Standards:** It can be helpful to relate data standards to associated business terms. This only relates to those business terms that describe specific data elements. And these data standards may not be applicable to every use of the attribute. Note any differences in the applicability of a standard.

- **Taxonomy classifications:** if your organization uses a taxonomy to classify or organize the business glossary or related aspects of the data catalog, attributes within the glossary should be made available to associate with appropriate business terms.

- **Related Ontologies:** Business terms may also be associated with any industry-specific ontologies used to control or organize related data.

- **Related Code Sets and Code Values:** Code sets and code values represent less extensive organizations of potentially controlled data sets. These may include US state abbreviations, Zip Codes, perhaps organizationally defined location codes, currency codes, or others.

Other industry code sets and classifications might be defined as something in between ontologies and code sets. These include many within healthcare, including:

- **ICD-10:** International Classification of Diseases, 10th Edition

- **HCPCS**: Health Care Common Procedure Coding System
- **CPT**: Current Procedure Terminology
- **CDT**: Code on Dental Procedures and Nomenclature
- **NDC**: National Drug Codes
- **DRG**: Diagnosis-related Group
- **NPI**: National Provider Identifier.

Some financial services code sets include:

- Stock ticker symbols
- Mutual fund tickers
- Standard international currency codes
- Standard Industrial Classification (SIC) codes used in filings to the Securities and Exchange Commission (SEC).

Taxonomies and ontologies

A data taxonomy is a methodology by which data is organized and classified into categories, subcategories, and attributes. Start with a simple taxonomy before implementing any data catalog, especially the data glossary. We cannot create a taxonomy for the entire organization's data until the data is understood by the team organizing the data dictionary and glossary.

Therefore, it makes sense to begin working through existing structures to organize the business glossary and data dictionaries.

If a business glossary exists, you can start there and add more categories and subcategories as you go on. data dictionaries and modern business glossary tools are flexible, so they can be modified and reorganized when the need arises. User Access can be adjusted regardless of the underlying organization by modifying views and dashboards, thus directing users to the subsets of data they need. Amazon didn't start by creating a product taxonomy that included all potential items they might sell, even based on the books they originally began with. Melvil Dewey could not imagine how all books could be organized when he created the Dewey decimal system. In fact, many libraries use his system in conjunction with other organizational methods by separating some types of books, like children's books, young adult books, mysteries, etc., by the author's last name. So, we can start with an organizational approach to our glossary and data dictionaries that makes sense for the information we start with while remaining flexible enough to allow for the additions of other categories, subcategories, and attributes.

Wikipedia defines an Ontology as encompassing "a representation, formal naming, and definitions of the categories, properties, and relations between the concepts, data, or entities that pertain to one, many, or all domains of discourse. More simply, an ontology is a way of showing the properties of a subject area and how they are related by defining a set of terms and relational expressions that represent the entities in that subject area."

This article continues by identifying Domain Ontologies, which refer to a specific area of knowledge and uses domain-specific language.

Reference

Wikipedia. *Ontology.*
https://en.wikipedia.org/wiki/Ontology_(information_science)

Ontologies can be used to provide greater formalization and structure to your data catalog and business glossary. Depending on your industry, you may want to relate specific data sets and data attributes to given industry ontologies. Examples of industry-focused ontologies include:

- Financial Industry Business Ontology (FIBO) which provides a common vocabulary for financial contracts and related concepts.
  https://github.com/edmcouncil/fibo

- SNOMED CT clinical terminology is a comprehensive, multilingual clinical healthcare terminology.
  https://www.snomed.org/what-is-snomed-ct

- Dublin Core Metadata Terms (DCMT) is a general-purpose metadata vocabulary for describing resources like those found online.
  https://www.dublincore.org/specifications/

- Gene Ontology (GO) provides a comprehensive, computational model of biological systems. https://geneontology.org/

- Chemical Entities of Biological Interest (ChEBI) "is a freely available dictionary of molecular entities focused on 'small' chemical compounds. ChEBI incorporates an ontological classification, whereby the relationships between molecular entities or classes of entities and their parents and/or children are specified." https://www.ebi.ac.uk/chebi/aboutChebiForward.do

- Dana Classification System of Mineralogy has provided a classification system for minerals since the mid-nineteenth century. https://www.cmnh.org/mineralogy/collection-database/dana-system

Technical Metadata

Technical metadata or data dictionary is what information technology professionals often think of first when they use the term "metadata." This metadata includes the information used by systems to structure and organize data. Here, we mainly discuss structured relational databases. There are many other types of information repositories, including multiple types of data like imaging, video, blobs, arrays, XML formatted data, JSON

formatted data, GIS mapping information, HTML, web, text
threads, social media feeds, etc. Therefore, many types of technical
metadata may describe, manage, and organize this information.
More information on more complex metadata approaches can be
found in books like "Developing Quality Metadata" by Cliff
Wootton. One of these initiatives is the Dublin Core Metadata
Initiative (DCMI), which was created to support documenting
web-based information. See https://www.dublincore.org/.

Technical metadata in a typical organization utilizing relational
database systems will include:

- Name of standard structures like databases, schemas,
  tables, database views, columns, files, and fields within
  files.

- High-level structural information, including database
  systems (Oracle, Snowflake, Microsoft SQL Server,
  Teradata, etc.) or file information such as CSV, TXT,
  XML, JSON, tab-delimited, etc.

- System information provides information on what
  systems or applications utilize the data structures.

- Connection information, such as the technical
  connection specifications identifying the database name,
  server name, file paths, etc.

- Descriptions for the above structures. These descriptions
  can be created at any point in database creation, whether

during modeling or later when documented in the data catalog or business intelligence toolset.

- Column-level metadata, including data type, nullability constraints, identification as primary or foreign keys, length (for string or certain numeric data types), and descriptions, if available.

- Data definition language, which can provide additional details for tables and views

- System and database logs can provide additional information related to database, system, and network events, access, and performance.

All of the above technical metadata can be made available for use in combination with business metadata recorded in the business glossary. This combination of technical and business metadata provides more value to an organization. A data dictionary pulled directly from database structures can provide information about the database's structures, design, and relationships. But, as noted above, these structures are designed for optimal data processing, not necessarily for optimal analytic potential or for "getting data out" for decision-making. Executives, managers, and analysts think in terms of business outcomes. They need to understand the valuable information collected in databases on their own terms. The combination of technical and business metadata provides that bridge.

Reference

Wootton, Cliff. (2009). *Developing Quality Metadata*. Routledge.

Challenges in documenting technical metadata include inaccessible data dictionaries from legacy systems (often the most important systems in established organizations); the variety of databases used to store, house, and manage data; complex data storage technologies, including those that are not instantiated in a physical manner, those created in a metadata-driven design, those housed in array-type structures; unstructured data including large text blocks or image, video, pdf or other types of formats; the sheer number of data sets existent across an organization.

In approaching data governance for the more obscure or difficult-to-access data repositories, it makes sense to prioritize the approach. In some cases, the organization may have created separate processes to access legacy data structures. It may be adequate to document these secondary data structures and move forward rather than either ignore high-value systems or spend extreme amounts of resources documenting the underlying metadata. An example of this I remember is a large banking system built in Cobol on a mainframe system. The organization created a reporting repository with a regular feed from the legacy system. This allowed not only reporting, but also the use of this data in messaging systems for other parts of the banking process. This repository became an integral part of the organization's systems. Since technical metadata was available to describe the data repository, it was less important to completely document data within the mainframe system.

Governance Metadata

Governance metadata includes metadata used to manage and govern data. Including governance metadata within the data catalog provides users with the ability to learn and understand expectations about the data, find the right people to ask questions, and learn about how data is managed within the organization. This is also where to place expectations and standards about how data is cataloged. It may be helpful to provide information on data architecture standards, naming conventions, data retention, and other standards relating to creating, managing, storing, and archiving data.

Governance metadata may include expectations about data quality. Augment this section with Chapter 7 on Data Quality Standards. Focus data standards on a variety of levels depending on organizational needs. Focus the initial expectations on different levels of data. The chart below provides some examples.

Data Level	Description	Example
Column	Standards for individual column data quality.	PATIENT_NAME should never be null.
Record	Standards for inserting records into the data repository (data lake, data warehouse, data marts, etc.).	Every record should include basic audit columns: CREATE_DATE, CREATED_BY, UPDATED_DATE, UPDATED_BY

Data Level	Description	Example
Data load	Standards related to each time data is loaded to the repository.	Each data load should include an audit check that all records are correctly loaded from the incoming data set to the repository table. If records are not loaded, reporting should be created, and an alert sent to a responsible party.
Naming Conventions	Provides naming standards for databases, schemas, tables, views, columns, relationships, etc.	Provides specific acceptable abbreviations for column and table names.
Metadata Standards	Document expectations for metadata to be collected and recorded about specific data elements.	Each database, schema, table, and column should include a meaningful description.
Applications	Provides standards related to how applications are documented within the organization.	All applications must have identified business and technical owners who verify related metadata on an annual basis.
AI/ML Models	Define how AI/ML models should be governed within the organization.	Any AI/ML models which are utilized in a productionalized manner must be documented within the data catalog.

Governance metadata also includes the identification of roles related to the creation, management, and control of data ownership of given data structures, subject matter experts for specific business terms or data sets, indicators for critical data elements (CDEs), or other pieces of information helpful to users, analysts and other stakeholders. Define roles in various ways depending on the organization's needs. Documenting the expectations for certain roles will help to ensure that people filling those roles understand their responsibilities, that people depending on others know what to expect, and that accountability can be achieved if responsibilities are not fulfilled. You can use various frameworks to work out data roles, including those defined in DAMA-DMBOK.

Governance metadata also includes the classification of data at a variety of levels. A high priority in modern data systems is classifying sensitive data, such as Protected Health Information (PHI) and Personally Identifiable Information (PII), as required by regulations such as GDPR and HIPAA. Data classification will be more important as more governments and regulatory organizations create rules around sensitive information. The identification of sensitive data should run from identifying systems with PHI/PII to identifying specific database columns. It should also include understanding where PHI/PII may be stored in non-structured data, such as large text fields. This is often a concern in healthcare systems where physicians, nurses, radiologists, pathologists, and other professionals create notes. Notes fields provide a high risk of exposure to sensitive data.

Other types of data classification include identifying and classifying data based on content and used to create meaning for analysts. As databases are often designed for optimum transactional performance rather than data export and analytics, naming is not a good indication of the actual content of a data structure. A good example of this challenge is the Enterprise Resource Planning (ERP) software SAP. SAP was designed and developed utilizing data structures named in German. English-speaking analysts may have difficulty identifying the content of data structures within SAP. Other challenges occur when individual columns may change over time or columns are just not named in a way that promotes data enablement. The content in a database may not be what the analyst expects. Automated classification using AI/ML may help allow "self-describing" addition of business metadata to a data dictionary. Again, tools like Collibra may help in this endeavor. Any support in adding business knowledge to a data dictionary is better than having many people manually tag metadata.

Reference

DAMA International. (2017). DAMA-DMBOK: Data Management Body of Knowledge. Second Edition. Technics Publications.

Process Metadata - Data Lineage

Ideally, data flows between systems, databases, tables, and columns should be documented and available to analysts, engineers, and auditors through the data catalog. Due to the processes, complexity, and constant change of data flows within a large organization, accessing and documenting these flows may be difficult or impossible. In my experience, I've not yet seen an organization able to document all data flows to the column level. This goal remains elusive but important. Not only do analysts and engineers need to know both the original source of data in data repositories and reporting, but many regulations, such as BCBS 239 and GDPR, require documentation of data processing and data quality, essentially data lineage documentation.

Reference

Steenbeek, Irina. *Data Lineage 103: Legislative requirements.* CFO.University. https://cfo.university/library/article/data-lineage-103-legislative-requirements-steenbeek

Within the catalog, data flows should include the following:

- Source data elements and associated position within the system (system, database, tables, columns, etc.).

- Target data elements and associated positions within the system (system, database, tables, columns, etc.).

- Logic is applied to data to extract or select the data set from the source system. Think of this as the outbound query.

- Transformations, including any logic applied to the data during processing. You can apply this logic at the data set level to select or transform the set as a whole. Or it may be at the attribute or column level.

- Technology, file structure, timing, and other specifics about how data is moved between structures

- Identification third-party if the source or target is external to the organization.

- Data transfer roles include subject matter experts and technical and business owners.

- Start and termination timestamps of implementation of data flows.

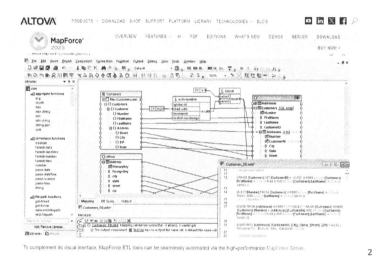

To complement its visual interface, MapForce ETL tools can be seamlessly automated via the high-performance MapForce Server.

2

Cataloged data lineage can be enhanced significantly by including dynamic, visual diagrams showing data flow. Many graphic-driven extraction, transformation and loading (ETL), and cataloging toolsets provide this approach to visualization of data flows. These diagrams provide the user with clickable interfaces that illustrate table-to-table and column-to-column, flows.

―――――――――――――――

2 ETL Mapping Software: ALTOVA.

Clicking on the various components of the diagram allows the user to see more details, including the actual code used to query data, filter, and move it to target structures.

Additionally, these tools allow both source and impact data analysis within systems. Examples include:

Source Analysis:

- Create a list of tables and columns which ultimately provide data for a specific column within a report.

- Tell me where this report column comes from in a given transactional system.

- Identify the logic used to calculate this column in the data warehouse.

Impact Analysis:

- Provide a list of all reports that may be impacted if the logic for a specific column is changed.

- Create a list of all tables that should be reviewed if a new column is added to data import to the data lake.

- List all structures which will be impacted if a major source system is decommissioned.

We will cover more details on implementing data lineage in Chapter 11 Data Lineage.

Process Metadata – Data Observability

So far, our discussion on data cataloging has focused on data at rest when data has stopped and is stored within systems and their associated databases. Data observability focuses on data in transition. It's important to remember that data constantly moves within and across systems. It's constantly changing. Data observability is focused on this fact. We'll cover more about data observability in another section of this book, but here, we are thinking about what information to include in the data catalog. Some information that might be helpful for catalog users includes the last created and last update dates for database structures and metadata. Information about processes like last data load timestamp, load row counts, frequency of updates or refreshes, failures, etc., might interest users.

CHAPTER 10

Master Data Management

Master data management (MDM) comes into play when a master data set becomes highly important to the organization and has become so complex that it must be managed separately. This complexity may be because the master data set is created and managed in multiple systems across the organization, it has become so large that one system cannot manage the details of the data set or that the data is needed in multiple systems and capacities but must also remain consistent and true across all the systems where it is used. MDM is more than a data store for one type of data. Mastered data is intended to be collected, managed, and then used across multiple platforms and systems within the organization.

As described above in the introductory sections, MDM can become complex and detailed. If you need to implement master data governance for one of your data domains, I highly recommend reading some of the books on the market about the subject, like "Master Data Management and Data Governance, 2nd Edition," by Alex Berson and Larry Dubov, prior to selecting MDM tools. While there are methods of resolving MDM issues using limited toolsets or "homegrown" solutions, MDM problem-solving usually requires a purchased solution. Many are on the market now, including Reltio, Informatica Intelligent Master Data Management Platform, TIBCO EBX, SAP Master Data Governance, and IBM InfoSphere Master Data Management.

Reference

Berson, A. and Dubov, L. (2010). Master Data Management and Data Governance, 2/E, 2nd Edition. McGraw-Hill.

After selecting a tool, your team should attend as much training as possible, reading vendor documentation, and taking any available computer-based training. MDM problems and solutions can be quite detailed and require a strong understanding of the data as well as the functionality of the toolset. As with other software implementations, solutions to specific business issues may not be immediately obvious or easily implemented. However, a strong understanding of the options within a tool and the potential resolutions on the business side can go a long way to successful implementation within an organization.

As noted earlier, MDM solutions are implemented to control and manage high-value entities within the organization's data. Customer is often the first entity to manage. The definition of customer will, of course, vary depending on the organization.

Patients, providers, clients, account holders, retirees, other businesses, employers, consumers, healthcare systems, government organizations, students, parents, schools, and non-profits could all be customers, depending on your business focus. Other important data entities may include products and services, locations, employees, partners, or inventories.

Berson and Dubov describe MDM as attempting to provide a "Single Version of Truth" regarding important business data entities. They point out that this does not always mean one physical record per entity but may require a "panoramic view of master data" depending on data owner needs. These authors provide support in creating a business case for the implementation of MDM for high-value data sets, including:

- Making improvements in sales, marketing, and business development success rates
- Reducing costs and increasing efficiencies in sales, marketing, and business development
- Improving risk management and compliance
- Improving customer service and customer experience
- Reducing operational costs of servicing customers.

These authors note that master data management is more than a tool-centered program. They point out that MDM must include a three-dimensional approach that includes a variety of organizational stakeholders (from front and back office through management and technology), the full lifecycle of any implementation (from planning through training), and depth of understanding (from awareness through buy-in and ownership). The authors also point out that the full solution within an organization may require multiple vendors as well as homegrown components. It's important to be open about solving these complex problems. After all, if the situation wasn't complex, we wouldn't need an MDM system to manage the data set.

Due to the intricacies and options for implementing master data management, we will not attempt to lay out the details of building an MDM system. Please refer to other texts for help in this regard. Rather, we'll lay out some of the considerations for MDM that a data governance program should include. This material is from "Master Data Management and Data Governance," by Berson and Dubov.

Data Synchronization

Data synchronization challenges often drive the need for MDM. These challenges occur due to many factors, some of which we've covered earlier. Synchronization issues may be caused by multiple systems collecting and providing attribute data about a given data entity where changes might need to be reviewed for contribution to the master record. Alternatively, various systems might collect different data attributes, which then need to be combined as part of the master record. Additionally, a variety of systems might need to be served with the master record, which may or may not correspond with the current system information for that entity.

For this reason, most MDM vendors provide the ability to create rules that allow the resolution of discrepancies between systems that provide data to the master record. Configure these rules to prioritize attributes from different source systems, support match and merge or suggest merger of multiple entity records into one, and identify relationships between data entities (families, hierarchies, subsidiaries, employer/employee, etc.).

Key MDM Capabilities

Berson and Dubov identify key capabilities that an MDM platform should support. These include:

- **Match/Merge/Unmerge Entity Resolution** provides the basis on which master data entities are identified as belonging to one real-world entity or one data entity, which can be broken into multiple records to reflect multiple real-world entities. This process should be rules-based and support a variety of approaches for identifying matching records.

- **Identifier Persistence** allows the MDM system to track the source of and synchronize updated master records with other systems.

- **Reconciliation, tracking, and arbitration of changes** allow for audit tracking as well as reversal of incorrect changes.

- **Data Security and visibility** controls access and visibility of highly sensitive data.

Also known as match/merge, entity resolution is one of an MDM platform's primary challenges and purposes. Berson and Dubov describe four types of algorithmic approaches to match/merge technology used by the major MDM vendors:

- **Deterministic algorithms:** utilize straightforward comparisons of individual attributes from different entities to identify matches. Examples of these attributes might include birth date, Social Security Number, names, etc. The benefits of this approach are its simplicity and speed. Deficiencies in this option include issues with misspellings, blank fields, abbreviations, and close matches.

- **Probabilistic algorithms:** apply statistical methods and weighted matching to identify equivalent entities.

- **Machine learning algorithms:** apply statistical methods along with artificial intelligence and machine learning to improve matching over time.

- **Hybrid algorithms:** use the above methods in combination with human intervention to achieve higher quality matching results.

The authors note that there are several factors involved in matching master records, especially in a large data environment:

- **Match accuracy** involves not only identifying true matches but also avoiding false positives. Obviously, different industries and use cases result in different tolerances for mistakes. For example, in healthcare, it's preferable to avoid sending patient results to the wrong patient. I've seen this become a serious issue in the case of twins with similar names.

- **Linking and matching speed** where it becomes important to quickly match existing records with new input. The authors use the example of a patient being admitted to the emergency room who requires a blood transfusion.

- **Persistence of the link keys** enables matched selections to be stored, validated, and passed to other systems for further processing.

- **Deterministic outcome** where the results should remain the same given the same inputs.

- **Scalability** ensures that the MDM system should be scalable enough to support the needs of the organization.

Here, it is important to know or be able to estimate future speed and throughput needs.

- **Ease of implementation and administration** enables the MDM platform to be implemented within the organization, with organization-based data, applied to the organization's master data challenges, but also integrates smoothly with the other systems within the organization's infrastructure. I've often seen an excellent vendor product not integrate well within the existing architecture and become untenable as a solution.

- **Flexibility** allows the solution to be changed to support changing business requirements. Berson and Dubov use the example of moving away from using social security numbers to protect customer privacy. The MDM administrator would need to configure the matching engine to avoid these attributes. We frequently see government regulations forcing unexpected changes to data management practices.

Planning for MDM Implementation

Implementing a master data management solution will require more analysis than this short chapter can recommend, but include the following items in planning.

Identify Target Data Domains

If you are just beginning to implement MDM within your organization, you will need to identify a finite set of data domains. Most frequently, the domains at highest risk for MDM issues include those related to customers (however your organization defines them) and products (again, as defined by your industry).

Document the use cases that must be managed by an MDM system and the issues and risks related to the data domains in question. Document the problems that need to be solved. Include information on internal and external systems related to the data domain. Which ones will provide master data and which will need to be fed by the MDM solution? Document the data flows required for these processes.

Identify the MDM architectural model required. Is this strictly focused on read-only analytical data, or is MDM required to support operational systems? What are the dependencies and timeframes required within the MDM environment?

Vendor Reviews

After documenting a high-level understanding of the need, research vendor options, ask for demonstrations, and obtain materials.

During this time, it will make sense to document details of data issues and expected correct solutions. Identify and document as many challenges as possible with existing data and systems. Document detailed requirements for the solution. These materials can be provided to vendors so they can prepare their responses. Creating a prioritized matrix of requirements can also be helpful. Additionally, it may be helpful to request either a "bake-off" where multiple vendors provide detailed demonstrations or request a demonstration period utilizing organizational data to test out capabilities.

Prototype Implementation

Identify a selective set of data to begin implementation. Work with your vendor to determine the best approach to implementation. This may create a parallel implementation to current mastering work to test the vendor toolset or utilize a smaller data set. Regardless, it is best not to implement a significant system like MDM with a "big bang" all-or-nothing approach. There is too much risk of failure or, at a minimum, of taking more time than the organization can afford to perfect the work.

Subsequent Implementations

Phases 2 plus can utilize the findings of the initial phase to improve implementation quality and speed. Take lessons learned and improve on the rules developed earlier, or add additional connections and capabilities. Again, I recommend working closely with your vendor to achieve optimum results.

CHAPTER 11

Data Lineage/Data Flows

As described earlier, data lineage allows the catalog user to understand how data moves through organizational systems and applications. These processes may be complex and interwoven, built up over years or decades of changes. Because many applications and databases may utilize data from other systems through a simple database connection or pick up flat files created for one purpose and use them without notifying the owners of the original system, there may be few records of how data moves through the hundreds of systems across a large organization. Simply identifying the existence of these data flows may be a challenge. Documenting the column-level flows and data transformations between systems is daunting. To date, we have seen limited success with utilizing automation to identify data flows and document these for users, management, and auditors.

Back in the day, and even now, we document data lineage and transformations using Excel spreadsheets. In the past, these have provided limited information on column-level lineage between systems. However, Excel documentation can be notoriously incomplete, inaccurate, and obsolete. Changes are often made within data-sharing processes that are not documented in the Excel mapping documents, changes are made during testing and implementation, and developers may not faithfully translate the mappings into code.

We need the ability to read data flows as implemented, not as planned. When looking at data flows at the column level, some catalog tools can read certain code sets like SQL, java, and dbt, and some extraction, transformation, and loading tools (ETL) like Informatica, Matillion, and Data Stage. Unfortunately, the catalog tool vendors are not interested in enabling the mapping of legacy technologies like COBOL from mainframe systems that are still in use, especially those that were niche even during the initial implementation. This is logical since enabling integration with older technologies can be expensive and time-consuming.

Furthermore, reading and understanding data movement can often be challenging when lineage can be read and documented within catalog tools. This is the point where visual diagrams can be helpful. Many ETL tools and catalog tools provide diagrams illustrating the column-to-column mappings between databases or between tables. This allows the analyst to understand movement more intuitively. Ideally, as catalog tools mature, these vendors will enable ways to provide data lineage information to users in more flexible ways, support integrations with more extraction, transformation, and loading tools, and allow ways to integrate older processes, such as those using messaging systems in addition to bulk loading tools.

Note that documenting data flow should include a variety of information, as noted in Chapter 9 on the data catalog. Therefore, simply reading SQL created to load tables from one database to another is not enough to show complete data lineage. Business-level questions are required to support technical, business, and regulatory expectations. We need to describe:

- What data is moving within, into, or out of organizational structures?
- How is this data selected?
- Why is this data moving?
- Who owns, manages, and understands the data being moved? Are they informed about the data flow? Are they willing to take responsibility for the data within the flow?
- How does the data move from one system to another?
- How is the data loaded to the target system?
- Who owns, manages, and understands the target system? Are they aware of any service level agreements for the data they are using?

Collect this information from a variety of sources, including documentation that may be created during design and implementation, information read from self-describing sources like ETL systems, and information that must be provided and maintained by technical and business owners.

A complete record of data flow may include:

- Data Flow Name
- Source System/Database/Schema/Table/Column
- Extract Query select statement
- Target System/Database/Schema/Table/Column
- Technology listing data file type, schedule, connection type
- Business Owner, Subject Matter Expert, Technical Owner
- Authorizations from the above stakeholders
- Column-to-column mapping and transformations
- Diagram of column-to-column mapping
- Start/End date of data flow.

Validate the above periodically or whenever implementing system changes.

CHAPTER 12

Purchased Data

Purchased, acquired, or external data can provide important information for an organization. Purchased data may include reference data sets, such as those required to maintain address quality, provide a complete set of comparative data for master data management such as the National Plan and Provider Enumeration System (NPPES) National Provider Identifier (NPI) directory for healthcare providers, data licensed from data marketing organizations, financial data sets from Bloomberg, Moody's or Dun and Bradstreet, industry sales figures (particularly applicable to the pharmaceutical industry), demographic, market research, etc. Purchased data may also include information shared via joint ventures or partner organizations.

Defining governance aspects of purchased or acquired data include:

- Limited control over data quality, change, and content.
- Limited access to metadata about purchased data.
- Limited flexibility of timing and timeliness of data updates.
- Cost of purchase or acquisition of data sets.
- Contract management for data purchases.
- Requirements of monitoring incoming data for changes, quality, and data observability issues.
- Compliance and legal considerations for the data purchaser.
- Potential risk of security breaches related to vendor data.
- Complexities of integrating purchased data with internal data.

While many of these challenges are consistent with those related to internally created and managed data sets, the purchasing organization has limited control of many aspects of external data creation. Larger data-selling vendors like Moody's, Dun and Bradstreet, and others provide even less flexibility for purchasers than related joint ventures or partners who might share data.

Incidents I've seen in my career include:

- Data elements that change without notice to the purchaser.
- Requests for data elements that exist in the original systems but require months of notice or expensive changes to obtain from the vendor or partner.

- Data quality issues which appear without notice and significantly affect the quality and usefulness of analytic results.
- Data connections and exchanges causing significant security breaches.
- Purchased data sets contracted for multiple units within the organization, duplicating costs with limited benefit.
- Misunderstood contractual limitations or requirements restricting the use of acquired data.
- Integration efforts with extensive complexity due to inconsistencies between the data sets.

To combat these challenges, I recommend a similar approach to that recommended for internal data, with some additional governance steps:

Inventory Purchased Data Sets: As usual, we start by documenting the scope of purchased data across the organization. This step may be challenging as much of this data may be purchased by individual departments, processed by individual staff members, or integrated into existing automation. Talk to a variety of departments across the organization, including those supporting reporting and analytic programs, executive reporting teams, finance and accounting, sales, marketing, IT integration teams, master data management teams, and even logistics and operations teams. Ask if they use data purchased, acquired, or shared from external organizations. Document the following:

- Third-party providing data. Contact information for the third party.
- Link or copy of the contract for shared data. Draw out any obligations the organization incurs by obtaining and utilizing this data. Identify any restrictions for the use and dissemination of acquired data.
- Any documentation of service level agreements (SLAs) related to the data.
- Frequency or periodicity of the acquired data. Periodicity relates to how often the vendor provides the data. What is the scheduled delivery frequency?
- Timeliness of the data. In this case, timeliness relates to how old the data is when provided.
- Data catalog and metadata for the data.
- A sample of the data, when available, or information on how to access a sample.
- Technical information on how the organization acquires the data in question.
- Name of an internal contact person who either understands the data or manages the relationship(s) with the vendor regarding the data sets.

Catalog External Data: This can be particularly helpful in organizations establishing a data catalog. This catalog can ultimately include internally created and managed data, internal data repositories, data shared from the organization to third parties, and, with the addition of purchased data, data originating from outside the organization and used within organizational systems. This provides a more complete picture of data across the organization. As with other data, we want to include both technical and business metadata about the external data sets. In addition, we can add information gathered in the inventory to provide metadata about the contract.

Integrate External Data to Lineage: If you implement data lineage analysis in your data governance, external data should be part of the documented flows. Obviously, lineage documentation will be next to impossible outside the boundaries of the organization. Therefore, lineage should start either where data is created within the organization or when the data first arrives in organizational systems. This first stop should be documented at the table/file and column/field levels if possible. This allows data lineage documentation to start at the element level and track each data element and data flow through subsequent stops in company systems.

Data Quality and Observability: Like internal data, external data can be monitored for data quality and data observability issues. Example monitoring might include:

- Conformance to expected delivery schedule and record counts
- Quality of critical data elements
- Change of data structures like new or deleted columns or new or missing tables
- Changes in completeness, like missing values for data elements.

For those data sets that are part of mission-critical data sets, send alerts to the appropriate staff as soon as problems are detected. In some cases, external data may need to be cleansed or transformed to integrate with existing organizational data. While this is normally not the best way to manage data quality issues (those should be corrected at the source), the constraints of acquired data make this necessary.

Monitoring and upkeep of metadata: As with internal and shared data, the inventory of acquired data should periodically be reviewed for any changes. At a minimum, the organization should create a process by which acquired data inventory items are reviewed and acknowledged on a periodic basis. The timing of these reviews should be determined based on the risk tolerance of the organization related to each type of data. Remove any obsolete data sets from the inventory, new ones added, and any changes to metadata made to the inventory.

CHAPTER 13

Externally Shared Data

M ost organizations share data outside the main organizational boundaries. This can include all types of data:

- Human resources (HR) data needed to support payroll and benefits.

- Licensed, sold, or shared transactional data that may provide value to other organizations like marketing groups, research organizations, vendors, or even related organizations.

- Financial service organizations may share data to further process transactions.

- Healthcare organizations may share data with government or public organizations to support healthcare monitoring for disease and outbreak prevention.

- Data is often shared with regulatory organizations, including governments and agencies to prove compliance processes.

- Finally, most modern organizations share data via the Internet with customers of all types, whether direct consumers or businesses that interact with consumers.

Data is at higher risk of exploitation when it moves outside the organization's firewalls. This exploitation may be in the form of inadvertent data disclosures when data is sent to the wrong person or hackers access data. While we want to protect all organizational data, especially sensitive data like personal health information (PHI), payment card information (PCI), personally identifiable information (PII), or confidential corporate information. But risks of disclosure increase for data intentionally placed outside the organization.

Therefore, we want to document and protect any data that is shared with outside parties. As many organizations are early in their data governance journey, creating an inventory of externally-shared data can be challenging. Ideally, we'd like the result to be an end-to-end lineage of incoming data created within the organization, with a column-level mapping to all data being shared outside the organization. That goal is just not practical in the short term and may never be accomplished. But every step along the way can add value. The following is a tactical guide to beginning governance of externally shared data.

Note that you may or may not want to include departments that share data directly with customers. Creating an inventory of all customer-facing external data sharing will increase the level of effort significantly but will ultimately result in a more inclusive inventory.

Also, note that the activity of identifying and documenting externally shared data can be a political challenge. Most staff members who are involved with delivering data to external parties are busy doing their jobs. They have created processes and systems to achieve the goals they are assigned, not inventorying and monitoring data. Assume that they are responsible for the safety and control of this data, but they may not think kindly of a data governance team dropping in to monitor their jobs. Executive support is sometimes required to encourage cooperation and communication from these teams.

Identify Departments that Share Data Externally: Identifying groups within a large organization that share data externally may be challenging. Begin with "the usual suspects":

- Human Resources

- Compliance

- Any groups set up to market, sell, license, or share data to organizations beyond the base customer group. This might include transactional information sold to marketers or research organizations.

- IT and business groups that use vendors who use organizational data to provide services back to the organization. As more IT work is outsourced to Software-as-a-service (SaaS) vendors, more data moves outside the organization and may be at risk.

- Joint ventures and corporate partners.

- Customer data portals and purchasing sites, including organizations that serve a "proxy" or organizational customers. In healthcare, these might include healthcare providers, employers, healthcare systems, healthcare payors, insurance companies, etc. In financial services, these might include employers, banks, investment firms, mutual funds, advisors, financial professionals in agencies, etc.

Inventory Data Sets: This step requires the departments who have been identified to provide lists of data shared outside the organization. As stated, we'd like a full inventory of data, including information about the actual data sets, such as source, tables/columns, timing of extracts, methods of extract and delivery, etc. But it can be quite difficult to collect this level of detail. Teams managing data-sharing activities may or may not keep good records relating to the data being shared. If they do, they may not store the attributes describing the data sets as a data governance team may want. Again, flexibility and executive support may be required to successfully create an inventory of data shared outside the organization.

Automate Data Inventories and Lineage: If possible, connect data catalog tools to the databases and transfer technologies used to move data from organizational systems to external parties. This can be achieved when those technologies are within the set of tools that the catalog can connect. For example, if customers and vendors access information directly from reporting tools like Tableau, Qlikview, or PowerBI, these reporting sets can be connected to the catalog and read at the column level, then have lineage read back to applicable databases. In many situations, this is not the case. Therefore, the organization must decide how much detail can and will be collected for an external shared data inventory. In the case of my last organization, we decided it was sufficient to identify each data set that was shared with external parties, not attempt to document to the column level.

Implement Data Profiling and Data Quality Analysis: As externally focused data can be at higher risk for creating issues with regulatory agencies, customers, contractual obligations, and reputational harm, it is important to monitor data quality for these data sets. As described in our Data Quality chapter, the process starts with profiling. Once profiling has been implemented, work with subject matter experts, analysts, and the data asset implementation team to identify data quality standards and rules that can be used to monitor ongoing data flows for data quality issues. Additionally, monitoring the data observability aspects of the data flows is important. These include, but are not limited to, timeliness of data flows, the volume of data, and trends of data quality dimensions such as completeness.

Provide Reporting and Access: Once detailed metadata has been collected, whether manually or electronically, it should be made available to appropriate staff. These may include compliance personnel, data governance staff, managers for applicable departments, etc. Reporting may be created utilizing a data catalog toolset or other manner of reporting either via data stored in a relational database system or some other inventory housed on Microsoft SharePoint or Confluence.

Monitoring and Upkeep: Obviously, the more automated the shared data inventory is, the easier it will be to maintain and keep current. At a minimum, the organization should create a process by which shared data set inventories are reviewed and acknowledged on a periodic basis. Determine the timing of these reviews based on the organization's risk tolerance related to each type of data. Remove any obsolete data sets from the inventory, new ones added, and any changes to metadata made to the inventory.

CHAPTER 14

Artificial Intelligence and Machine Learning

A rtificial Intelligence and Machine Learning strongly depend on data governance due to using existing data in models. This chapter introduces how to manage data governance and AI together.

There are many opportunities within business and technology to utilize Machine Learning (AI/ML). Examples of AI projects in banking include:

- Royal Bank of Canada (RBC) utilizes AI-enabled "data-driven insights to help retail customers better manage their finances by tracking spending, automating budgeting, suggesting opportunities for savings, and forecasting future cash flow".

- RBC also "Traders and AI scientists worked side-by-side to deliver a real-world solution through the launch of Aiden® and the subsequent launch of Aiden Arrival – using deep reinforcement learning to navigate dynamic market conditions in real-time in its pursuit of improved trading results and insights for clients."

- ING is "providing a better customer experience and whether I do that via open finance or using generative AI in our call centres. Or utilizing the blockchain to tokenize mortgages and provide them in five days, rather than 60 days."

The US National Institutes for Health (NIH) report the following, including experimental and current uses for AI/ML in healthcare:

- Electronic Health Record (EHR) data being used for predicting diagnoses.

- "Predicting post-stroke pneumonia using deep neural network approaches."

- "Chronic disease prediction using medical notes."

- "Pneumonia detection on Chest X-Rays with Deep-Learning"

In October 2024, the Nobel Prize for Chemistry went to developers of AlphaFold AI, which was used to predict protein structures.

Reference

Madhvi, Sonia. (2023, November 20). *AI: Here's what every bank in the world is working on.* Finextra.com. https://www.finextra.com/the-long-read/866/ai-heres-what-every-bank-in-the-world-is-working-on

Habehh, H. and Gohel, S. (2021, December 16). *Machine Language in Healthcare.* Current Genomics. https://www.ncbi.nlm.nih.gov/pmc/articles/PMC8822225/

Callaway, Ewen. (2024, October 9). *Chemistry Nobel goes to developers of AlphaFold AI that predicts protein structures.* Nature. https://www.nature.com/articles/d41586-024-03214-7.

Types of AI/ML Models

There are several types of machine learning and algorithms. Below is a short introduction. Any data governance practitioner who expects to help govern AI products or services should research the subject in more detail.

- **Supervised Learning**: where the algorithm is provided labels via a "training" set of data. The algorithm then "learns" to classify the labels that should be applied to the remaining data set. Think of the CAPTCHA and ReCAPTCHA tools used to identify whether a web user is a robot or a human. We identify images to provide the system with more training data and prove we are not robots.

- **Unsupervised Learning:** In this type of machine learning, the algorithm must utilize the characteristics and attributes within the data set to detect groupings and patterns in the data but not provide training data. Examples include recommendation tools like those utilized by Amazon, Facebook, and LinkedIn to identify content that may interest users based on interests or purchases by similar users. Additionally, use unsupervised learning to detect anomalies. Banks and financial institutions may use this type of ML algorithm to detect fraud.

- **Reinforcement Learning**: Reinforcement Learning algorithms can use a combination of both supervised and unsupervised learning but often have the model results enhanced by humans or other types of validation. Examples of reinforcement learning algorithms can be seen in self-driving cars, automated machinery, natural language processing (NLP), and healthcare applications with diagnosis and treatment recommendations. Think of this as the way you train your dog. If the dog does the right thing, he gets a treat. If he doesn't, no reward is provided. Eventually, he self-adjusts to obtain the treat more frequently.

- **Deep Learning:** Uses more sophisticated methods to create artificial neural networks that can utilize the above types of algorithms. Examples of deep learning and neural networks include facial recognition systems, chatbots, and more sophisticated recommender systems. Deep learning advancements have led to generative AI and natural language processing using Large Language Models (LLMs).

- **Large Language Models:** Deep-learning models trained with vast amounts of language data, such as that available on public internet sites and social media. These models have revolutionized AI acceptance by the public. ChatGPT, autocomplete, and other similar applications are examples of technologies based on LLMs.

- **Generative AI**: Includes technologies built utilizing deep learning applied to a variety of media, including text-based language, but also including image, audio, and video. ChatGPT is a text-based example of GenAI, but other tools enable the generation of images, video, music, 3D imaging, and robotics.

Governing AI/ML

Two aspects of data governance relate to artificial intelligence and machine learning (AI/ML). These are governing AI/ML models and projects and governing the data that support AI/ML. These are not mutually exclusive, but the differences can be used as a jumping-off point for discussion. The explosion of interest in AI/ML has made it imperative to incorporate these technologies in any data-related planning and activities. Consumers, customers, and shareholders insist that AI be considered in products and services. At the same time, the use of AI/ML also makes it imperative that data is of the highest quality to achieve the most accurate results. Unfortunately, the quality of data used within AI models is not always at the level data scientists require. Additionally, AI/ML models may not be governed and managed in a way that protects users, consumers, customers, and the public from ill intentions, naïve mistakes, or changes to either the underlying data set or model learnings that change results (drift). Additionally, governments and organizations are introducing regulations and requirements for stricter governance over AI/ML models and associated data sets, whether these sets are used as sources for the models or are part of data resulting from applying AI/ML models.

Two aspects of data governance relate to artificial intelligence and machine learning (AI/ML). These govern AI/ML models and projects and the data supporting AI/ML.

AI Drift

Model drift refers to the degradation of machine learning model performance due to changes in data or in the relationships between input and output variables. Model drift, also known as model decay, can negatively impact model performance, resulting in faulty decision-making and bad predictions.

Reference

IBM. *What is model drift?* IBM. https://www.ibm.com/topics/model-drift

As with other chapters of this book, we cannot capture every aspect of AI/ML data governance nor assume that you use a specific organizational model for AI/ML governance. Your organization may create a specific team to manage AI/ML and related governance, or work may occur within the data governance department or another department like IT Security or Compliance.

However these tasks are accomplished, the intent here is to provide an overview of activities required to begin governance of AI/ML models as well as the data that is used as inputs to these models and data that results from applying AI/ML technologies. Also, remember that these technologies are evolving rapidly, and attempts here to nail down specifics will likely become outdated quickly.

Inventory AI/ML Models within the Org

As with any data governance topic, we should start with documenting the scope of AI/ML activities within the organization. As AI is relatively new, it may be easier to identify all teams and departments utilizing AI/ML technologies now than it will be once these techniques become integral to all IT toolsets.

As these tools become part of more applications and platforms, it will become more difficult to identify and document the use of AI. An inventory should be created and maintained to list AI/ML projects and models used across the organization. This inventory should include:

- Model Name
- Model Description
- Purpose
- Ownership by department and named resource
- Audience/customer
- Third-party involvement (including development vendors or consuming organizations)
- Technologies and toolsets employed
- Risks
- Controls
- Use of sensitive data sets like PHI, PII, PCI, and data covered by regulations such as GDPR, CCPA, and AI regulations
- Testing approach (both for implementation and ongoing to avoid inappropriate drift)
- Regulatory concerns related to the toolset, data, consumers, users, etc.

Risk Management for Artificial Intelligence

Because AI/ML creates additional risk for organizations, risk management activities should be created that specifically review these concerns. In some organizations, these risk management reviews and management may occur within the regulatory compliance organization, the technology teams, the data governance organization, or a new department specifically created for AI/ML.

In 2019, Ernst & Young, LLP published a helpful document on "Building the right governance model for AI/ML," specifically targeting the financial services sector. E&Y recommends the following steps for AI/ML model governance:

1. **Develop an enterprise-wide AI/ML definition**: E&Y notes that the wide-ranging application of AI technology can make it difficult to identify use cases. Documenting an approach to identifying what applications are or are not AI/ML will help.

2. **Enhance existing risk management and control frameworks to address AI/ML-specific risks**: As the authors note, existing programs like "model risk management (MRM), data management (including privacy), compliance and operational risk management (IT risk, information security, third-party, cyber)" can be modified to include issues related to AI/ML. Approach

these modifications and governance of AI/ML models in a cross-functional manner.

3. **Implement an operating model for responsible AI/ML adoption**: E&Y recommends implementing appropriate oversight committees and reporting structures along with Centers of Excellence (CoEs) that may vary from activity-creating AI/ML models to only providing oversight and guidance, depending on the organization's needs.

4. **Invest in capabilities that support AI/ML adoption and risk management**: E&Y recommends an approach that includes AI/ML investments as part of strategic planning and risk management. This aligns with the current technology environment, which heavily emphasizes AI/ML, large language models (LLMs), and Generative AI. These investments include products, services, and processes that utilize AI and ML.

Once an inventory of existing AI/ML projects and models has been created and associated monitoring and control activities have been defined, existing and new projects should be reviewed according to risk-level standards. Any deficiencies identified during these reviews should be resolved and retested based on organizational standards for implementing audit findings.

Reference

Ernst & Young LLP. (2019). *Building the right governance model for AI/ML.* Building the right governance model for AI/ML (pdf)

Cataloging AI/Models

After documenting the AI/ML models, you can add them to the data catalog. AI models can be added as separate asset classifications within most of the current catalog tools. Include the attributes listed above for the inventory in cataloged metadata. Additionally, models can be associated with the data sets that provide data, including all the relevant technical metadata down to columns or attributes, linked together utilizing data lineage mapping, including information on transformations and logic used to manipulate source data before the model, and may include information about training data sets, requirements of the model design, etc. Including AI models in a data product marketplace can help data users identify potentially useful tools for application to new problems and situations.

Challenges of Governing AI/ML

Artificial intelligence and Machine Learning present specific challenges that are not readily apparent in standard database and data management technologies. The National Institute of

Standards and Technology provides a strong Artificial Intelligence Risk Management framework.

Some challenges described in the framework include:

- **Opacity of Output:** Due to the complexity of programming in creating artificial intelligence solutions, these systems may appear as "black boxes" to users and implementation teams. This can be particularly challenging with technologies utilizing deep learning and neural networks. These technologies are difficult to understand, but auditing inputs and results can often be more difficult. Here, the difference is between creating a report using specific SQL-based logic, filters, and transformation logic, or inputting a question to ChatGPT, which may reply with different results over time.

- **Training and Development Data Quality and Representation:** Data sets used for training and implementation should be large but representative of data expected to be used within the model in the future. Examples of facial recognition systems that do not provide accurate results for darker-skinned people have been made public. These deficiencies can lead to compliance, conduct, and legal risks.

- **Regulatory Changes:** Organizations planning to implement AI/ML technologies must be aware that governments are implementing new regulations to govern the use and implementation of AI. Many US States and countries are implementing new laws and regulations. For example, the European Union's Artificial Intelligence Act (EU AI Act) was signed into law in 2024. Organizations utilizing AI/ML technologies must keep appraised of changes in the regulatory environment.

- **Verification and ongoing testing**: While organizations should test AI models and software upon initial implementation, the dynamic nature of these tools requires continual monitoring and testing to guard against unexpected changes, unexpected inputs, drift, and potential misuse.

- **Third-party involvement** in AI development, including software, hardware, and data, complicates the organization's ability to identify, track and manage risk. If the organization purchases AI solutions from a third-party vendor, they don't have direct access to software development, testing, training, and deployment information. If an organization develops AI models for other organizations, they may not have control of uses, which may or may not align with expected risk management strategies.

- **Audiences** may affect the risks involved in utilizing AI/ML technologies. Those technologies used internally within a given organization may not incur the risks associated with those applied to public-facing systems. AI tools utilized solely within an organization may be used differently when sold to a third party. Additional risk assessment and testing should occur when a technology is used with a new audience. The NIST AI framework calls out the need to assess AI technologies in context. A new audience may utilize an AI tool in a way that is not expected by initial implementors. Testing should be robust and involve multiple audience groups.

- **Trustworthiness** in AI/ML models requires appropriate development methodologies, a strong testing approach, and monitoring throughout the lifecycle of the product. NIST discusses trustworthiness in their AI Framework: validation, reliability, accuracy and robustness or generalization.

- **Safety** requires that AI systems not "under defined conditions, lead to a state in which human life, health, property, or the environment is endangered."

- **Secure and resilient** characteristics are related to safety. Secure AI systems should not be open to "adversarial examples, data poisoning, and the exfiltration of models, training data, or other intellectual property through AI endpoints." Resilience is "the ability to return to normal function after an unexpected adverse event."

- **Fairness** requires that AI systems are built in a way that protects against harmful bias and discrimination. Additionally, systems should be accessible to everyone with a reason for use, including those with disabilities.

Reference

National Institute for Standards and Technology, US Department of Commerce. (2023, January). *Artificial Intelligence Risk Management Framework (AI RMF 1.0)*. NVL Pubs NIST Gov. https://nvlpubs.nist.gov/nistpubs/ai/NIST.AI.100-1.pdf

The White House. *Blueprint for an AI Bill of Rights*. https://www.whitehouse.gov/ostp/ai-bill-of-rights/

European Commission. (2024). *Shaping Europe's Digital Future*. Digital-Strategy.EC.Europa.eu. https://digital-strategy.ec.europa.eu/en/policies/regulatory-framework-ai

World Economic Forum. (2024, September 5). *AI governance trends: How regulation, collaboration, and skills demand are shaping the industry*. World Economic Forum. https://www.weforum.org/agenda/2024/09/ai-governance-trends-to-watch/

Financial Stability Board. (2017, November 1). *Artificial intelligence and machine learning in financial services*. Financial Stability Board. https://www.fsb.org/2017/11/artificial-intelligence-and-machine-learning-in-financial-service/

Measuring Data Quality for AI/ML

As recommended in the chapter on data quality, measure data quality before using in models by running profiling processes to identify the existing content of source data for models. Utilizing these measurement processes continuously is intended to ensure that incoming data does not change in essential quality. Implement measurements and profiling on data created by the AI model to ensure that results do not drift from those established after implementation. Assume that models will drift and may collapse even if initial testing produces appropriate results.

Data Governance and Artificial Intelligence

While data governance can help improve data quality and data use for data going into and emerging from AI systems, AI governance must account for special aspects of AI/ML technologies not usually seen in standard data governance implementations. These aspects include the current exponential growth of new AI/ML models, algorithms, and uses. They also include allowance for AI as a "learning" technology. The same inputs do not always result in the same outputs. The "Black Box" aspect of AI technology requires special attention to how the technology changes over time. We must continue to monitor these tools, not assume that the results in the original implementation will continue to be accurate as the toolset is used over time.

CHAPTER 15

Regulatory Data Governance

R egulatory risks can be the most consequential of all the reasons for enacting data governance within an organization. When an organization is found guilty of regulatory non-compliance, costs can mount quickly, including legal fees, regulatory fines, consumer suits, reputational loss, and even potential jail time. Even if an organization can negotiate a settlement with a regulatory authority, audit requirements may continue for years afterward to ensure future compliance. Overall, the costs of failing to manage regulatory risk related to data management can be high.

An additional concern is the continual change in the regulatory environment around data, which includes a new focus on how organizations utilize AI/ML and Generative AI technologies. An organization must be aware of changes to the regulatory environment with respect to all aspects of the data it creates, shares, receives, manages, and disseminates. Earlier sections of this text discussed some of the predominant data-focused regulations, including HIPAA, GDPR, CCPA/CCRA, and FERPA. Additional regulations related to the use of AI/ML are coming to the forefront. Many national and state organizations are writing and passing laws on the creation, use, management, and transparency of AI/ML technologies. These laws will naturally affect how data governance is implemented within organizations that utilize these technologies.

The European Union Artificial Intelligence Act (AI Act)

Four-point summary:

- The AI Act classifies AI according to its risk.

- The majority of obligations fall on providers (developers) of high-risk AI systems.

- Users are natural or legal persons who deploy an AI system in a professional capacity, not affected end-users.

- General purpose AI (GPAI) All GPAI model providers must provide technical documentation, instructions for use, comply with the Copyright Directive, and publish a summary of the content used for training.

Reference

(2024, February 27). EU Artificial Intelligence Act: High-level summary of the AI Act. https://artificialintelligenceact.eu/high-level-summary/

In addition to tracking relevant regulations based on jurisdictional applicability, an organization should document and manage required activities for each regulation. Overall, there are consistent expectations that many of these laws and regulations have in common. These include:

- **Tracking**: Inventory and document various aspects of data collection, management, and use, including data sets, personal data, health information, and AI/ML technologies. For example, CCPA requires organizations to identify what personal data elements are collected about consumers and for what purposes those data elements are used.

- **Transparency:** Communicate how data is used, how systems like AI work, and how reporting is calculated. For example, BCBS 239 encourages financial institutions to create reports that are well documented in terms of both definitions (a dictionary), accurate (in terms of data quality), and correctly aggregated (lineage).

- **Party Identification:** Know Your Customer, Anti-Money Laundering, and the US Patriot Act, among others, require financial institutions to be able to identify customers, the customer's authorizations to use accounts or make certain transactions, and to report on transactions and accounts based on specific rules and laws. Other types of organizations are covered by sanction laws, which also establish the need to identify customers accurately. There is a need for strong master data management over party data, including customer, patient, client, account, product, and other subject areas.

- **Flexibility:** These regulations and the ever-changing market climate require an organization to manage data in ever-changing economic, social, and business environments. BCBS speaks significantly to the need for banks to be able to manage risk management data and the risks this data reflects during crises. Establishing a strong data governance infrastructure, including data and business dictionaries, data quality management, master data management, and data lineage feeding into reporting.

- **Comprehensiveness:** While we need to start somewhere, a strong data governance infrastructure should ultimately cover the most significant aspects of an organization's business. The regulations reviewed in this text all point to the need for a risk-based approach to data governance where the most important and highest-risk aspects of the business are covered completely. Here, we are reminded that data governance is not just a data catalog or data lineage but also a full view of data management across the organization.

BCBS 239

The Basel Committee on Banking Supervision's standard number 239 was published in January 2013 to apply to all Global Systematically Important Banks (G-SIBs) after the financial crises of 2008 and beyond. BCBS 239 includes basic principles including:

Overarching Governance and Infrastructure

- **"Governance**: A bank's risk data aggregation capabilities and risk reporting practices should be subject to strong governance arrangements consistent with other principles and guidance established by the Basel Committee."

- **"Data architecture & IT Infrastructure**: A bank should design, build, and maintain data architecture and IT infrastructure that fully supports its risk data aggregation capabilities and risk reporting practices not only in normal times but also during times of stress or crisis while still meeting the other Principles."

- **"Accuracy & Integrity**: A bank should be able to generate accurate and reliable risk data to meet normal and stress/crisis reporting accuracy requirements. Data should be aggregated on a largely automated basis to minimize the probability of errors."

- **Completeness**: Including the ability to produce timely risk information when appropriate, knowing what risk information needs to be available at what timing, and acknowledging that "certain risk data may be needed faster in a stress/crisis situation."

- **Timeliness**: A bank should be able to generate aggregate and up-to-date risk data in a timely manner while also meeting the principles relating to accuracy, integrity, completeness, and adaptability.

- "**Adaptability**: A bank should be able to generate aggregate risk data to meet a broad range of on-demand, ad hoc risk management reporting requests, including requests during stress/crisis situations, requests due to changing internal needs and requests to meet supervisory queries."

Risk Reporting Practices

- **Accuracy**: Risk management reports should accurately and precisely convey aggregated risk data and reflect risk in an exact manner. Reports should be reconciled and validated.

- "**Comprehensiveness**: Risk management reports should cover all material risk areas within the organization. The depth and scope of these reports should be consistent with the size and complexity of the bank's operations and risk profile, as well as the requirements of the recipients."

- **Clarity & Usefulness**: Risk management reports should communicate information clearly and concisely. Reports should be easy to understand yet comprehensive enough to facilitate informed decision-making. Reports should include meaningful information tailored to the needs of the recipients.

- **Frequency**: The board and senior management (or other recipients as appropriate) should set the frequency of risk management report production and distribution. Frequency requirements should reflect the recipient's needs, the nature of the risk reported, the speed at which the risk can change, and the importance of reports in contributing to sound risk management and effective and efficient decision-making across the bank. Increase the frequency of reports during times of stress/crisis.

- **Distribution** – Distribute risk management reports to the relevant parties while maintaining confidentiality.

Reference

Basel Committee on Banking Supervision. (2013, January). *Principles for effective risk data aggregation and risk reporting.* www.bis.org. https://www.bis.org/publ/bcbs239.pdf

Uniting and Strengthening America by Providing Appropriate Tools Required to Intercept and Obstruct Terrorism (USA PATRIOT) Act of 2001

The purpose of the USA PATRIOT Act is to deter and punish terrorist acts in the United States and around the world, to enhance law enforcement investigatory tools, and other purposes, some of which include:

- To strengthen US measures to prevent, detect, and prosecute international money laundering and financing of terrorism;

- To subject to special scrutiny foreign jurisdictions, foreign financial institutions, and classes of international transactions or types of accounts that are susceptible to criminal abuse;

- To require all appropriate elements of the financial services industry to report potential money laundering;

- To strengthen measures to prevent the use of the US financial system for personal gain by corrupt foreign officials and facilitate repatriation of stolen assets to the citizens of countries to whom such assets belong.

Reference

Financial Crimes Enforcement Network. *USA PATRIOT ACT.* www.fincen.gov.
https://www.fincen.gov/resources/statutes-regulations/usa-patriot-act

FINRA Rule 2090 Know Your Customer

.01 Essential Facts. For purposes of this Rule, facts "essential" to "knowing the customer" are those required to (a) effectively service the customer's account, (b) act in accordance with any special handling instructions for the account, (c) understand the authority of each person acting on behalf of the customer, and (d) comply with applicable laws, regulations, and rules.

Reference

FINRA. *2090. Know Your Customer.* www.finra.org.
https://www.finra.org/rules-guidance/rulebooks/finra-rules/2090

CHAPTER 16

Privacy, Access, and Identity Management

This chapter provides a high-level overview of topics integral to data governance but cannot be covered completely in a short chapter. We will attempt to provide enough information to guide your work in this area. If your team is working through issues related to data access governance, please do further research in both related books and literature but with the applicable vendors. Data access, data privacy, and access management are changing quickly. New AI capabilities are being added for data classification, access controls, access monitoring, and other aspects of these topics. Some of the material in this chapter has been collected by vendors in this area, but the capabilities of these tools are changing quickly, so the tools will be changing over time.

Palo Alto Networks provides a good overview of data access governance.

Data access governance is a strategic component of data governance. It involves the processes and technologies organizations use to manage, monitor, and control access to their data. The primary goal of data access governance is to ensure that the right people have the right access to the right data at the right time while also safeguarding sensitive information from unauthorized access.

Reference

Paloalto Networks. *What is Data Access Governance?* Paloaltonetworks.com. https://www.paloaltonetworks.com/cyberpedia/data-access-governance

Keep in mind that data access governance applies to data across an organization's complete environment, including:

- data housed on owned hardware
- all data across cloud-based infrastructure
- data used by the organization on products supported by vendors as software-as-a-service (SaaS)
- "shadow data" where data has been extracted from controlled environments for backups, desktop models, Excel analysis, AI modeling, or other uses,
- data received from external parties
- data shared with external parties.

Data access governance includes the following activities:

- **Data Discovery:** Identify and classify sensitive data based on regulatory and organizational requirements.

- **Access Controls:** Design policies and procedures and utilize technologies that limit access to appropriate users/systems for appropriate activities at appropriate times.

- **Data Anonymization:** Where applicable, data should be anonymized using appropriate technologies to avoid sharing with unauthorized parties.

- **Monitoring**: Control access to all data by users, applications, and systems, understanding which allows permission to view, modify, or delete data of various sensitivities.

- **Maintain reporting and audit capabilities:** To detect potential violations and provide regulatory and audit details for both the design and results of data access implementations.

Data Access Governance Technologies

Software products used for data access governance include some or all the following technologies. Some of these may overlap depending on the vendor and organizational approach:

- **Data Security Posture Management (DSPM)** solutions provide comprehensive visibility into sensitive data assets, roles, and permissions across multiple cloud environments. They also help prioritize and manage access risks and streamline governance-related tasks. Some solutions incorporate DSPM into a broader data security platform.

- **Identity and Access Management (IAM)** tools enable organizations to manage user identities, access controls, and permissions across various systems and applications. They're used to revoke or grant permissions but aren't contextually aware of the data stored in each cloud resource. Examples include Okta, Azure Active Directory, and AWS Identity and Access Management (IAM).

- **Data Loss Prevention (DLP)** solutions focus on preventing data leakage, whether intentional or accidental. They monitor, detect, and block sensitive data transmission, often incorporating data access governance features to help manage access to sensitive data.

- **Data Access Controls (DAC)** are a subset of identity and access management that focus on how users and systems are allowed access to specific data sets.

- **Database Activity Monitoring (DAM)** refers to a suite of tools that can be used to support the ability to identify and report fraudulent, illegal, or other undesirable behavior with minimal impact on user operations and productivity. The tools have evolved from basic analysis of user activity in and around relational database management systems (RDBMSs) to encompass a more comprehensive set of capabilities, such as discovery and classification, vulnerability management, application-level analysis, intrusion prevention, support for unstructured data security, identity, and access management integration, and risk management support.

https://www.paloaltonetworks.com/cyberpedia/data-access-governance

Reference

Gartner. *Database Activity Monitoring (DAM)*. Gartner.com. https://www.gartner.com/en/information-technology/glossary/database-activity-monitoring-dam

Data Access Risks

According to IBM's website, the following risks exist for improper data access management:

- **Misconfigurations** where security settings are missing or incomplete, leaving data vulnerable to unauthorized access. These can often be found in cloud data implementations, unapplied security patches, or in missed data encryption setups.

- **Overentitlements** are where users are allowed more data access than is needed to perform their jobs. Overentitlements may occur due to poor administration of least-access principals, temporary rights not revoked in a timely manner, or simply the result of misconfiguration.

- **Data Flow and Lineage-Related Issues** as data is moved between organizational systems, data access controls may change based on data processing needs within each system or repository. Understanding data lineage throughout organizational systems, including into and outside the organization, is a priority for a thorough approach to DPSM.

- **Security Policy and Regulatory Violations** DSPM solutions map the data's existing security settings to the organization's data security policies—and to the data security requirements mandated by any regulatory frameworks to which the organization is subject—to identify where data is inadequately protected and where the organization runs the risk of non-compliance.

Reference

IBM. *What is data security posture management (DSPM)?* IBM.
https://www.ibm.com/topics/data-security-posture-management

Sensitive Data Discovery

Many vendors across the data governance toolscape say they enable automated discovery of data classification and sensitive data identification. This capability is sorely needed because manual identification of all columns and fields with potential privacy requirements is time-consuming and fraught with potential for error. Additionally, relying on database tables and column naming conventions to identify the content of data has a high potential for missing important elements. How often do developers, application users, and analysts rename columns, use columns for multiple purposes, or simply ignore naming requirements to get data into a system?

Large text-based columns like note fields and other open fields allow for private information or identifiable data elements to appear unexpectedly when an attempt has been made to de-identify or mask data. Accurate automated data classification of sensitive data, such as PHI, PII, PCI, etc., must rely on data content, not strictly metadata (column names). AI/ML models utilizing natural language processing (NLP) and large language models (LLMs) will become the gold standard for these classification engines.

Data Access Control Models

According to Sailpoint, one of the vendors of IAM/DAC products, there are four main models for applying data access control:

- **"Discretionary Access Control (DAC):** The least restrictive data access control model, DAC relies on the owner or administrator of the resource to decide who has access permission. This decentralized model allows users to share access with others, making it difficult to oversee who is accessing your company's sensitive information.

- **Mandatory Access Control (MAC):** In this nondiscretionary model, the end-user has no control over the permission settings. A central authority, such as an administrator or owner, controls the access, setting, changing, and revoking permissions.

- **Role-Based Access Control (RBAC):** Access in this model is granted based on a set of permissions, which depend on the level of access that user categories need for performing their day-to-day duties. With RBAC, different roles receive different access privileges based on criteria such as job function and responsibilities. A widely used system, RBAC combines role assignments with authorizations and permissions. It's designed around predetermined roles, defined by criteria such as cost center, business unit, individual responsibilities, and authority. When a person changes responsibilities, jobs, or functions, the administrator assigns that user a new role that's predefined in the system.

- **Attribute-Based Access Control (ABAC):** A dynamic data access control model, ABAC grants access based on both attributes and environmental conditions, which include factors such as location and time. These attributes and conditions are assigned both to the users and the data or other resources. ABAC provides more flexibility than RBAC because you can modify the attributes and their values without having to change the subject/object relationships. That means that when you make new decisions about access, you can dynamically change the access controls."

Reference

SailPoint. *What is data access control?* SailPoint. https://www.sailpoint.com/identity-library/what-is-data-access-control

---

Principle of Least Privilege

The principle is that a security architecture should be designed so that each entity is granted the minimum system resources and authorizations that the entity needs to perform its function.

Reference

Nieles, M, Dempsey, K. and Pillitteri, V. Y., (2017, June). *An Introduction to Information Security*. NVLpubs.nist.gov. https://nvlpubs.nist.gov/nistpubs/SpecialPublications/NIST.SP.800-12r1.pdf

Data Anonymization

In addition to restricting access to data via the above models (MAC, RBAC, ABAC), data can be anonymized for various purposes. Some of these include utilizing sensitive "production" level data during development activities (particularly when development occurs in countries with restricted data authorization), sharing de-identified data with third parties for research and marketing purposes, or collecting data from customers without consent but used for specific purposes allowed by regulations like GDPR.

The International Association of Privacy Professionals (IAPP) provides a guide to anonymization that describes the basic types of anonymization techniques. Please conduct further reading on this topic should you need to implement anonymization in your organization.

Attribute Suppression: removes attributes of the data set, usually columns, to remove sensitive information. For example, removing the name or Social Security Number from a personal record. The column should be completely removed, not hidden or redacted.

Character Masking: by hiding characters with another character, X for example. A simple example is where a Social Security Number is masked on a bank account web page.

Pseudonymization: replaces identifying data with replacement values. Depending on the process used, pseudonyms may or may not be reversible.

Generalization: summarizes data in a way that intentionally reduces the precision of data. Examples include creating age ranges or using fewer digits of a Zip Code for location.

Swapping: rearranging data in a way that the individual attributes remain in the data set but do not correspond to the original records. Also called shuffling or permutation.

Data Perturbation: when values that may be semi-identifying are changed slightly by adding rounding or random noise.

Synthetic Data: a technique that creates realistic data that does not reflect actual sensitive data. This type of anonymization can be used to create data for development or testing activities. It may also be called "test" data.

Data Aggregation: uses statistical techniques, summaries, or aggregations to remove sensitive data details.

Use these techniques separately or together to ensure that data use does not contradict organizational or regulatory requirements for certain uses, such as shared data for research or marketing. Additionally, when combined with data access controls, anonymization, and masking can limit internal exposure of sensitive data to employees without the need to view data.

Reference

Personal Data Protection Commission. Singapore. (2018, January 25). *Guide to Basic Data Anonymisation Techniques.* IAPP.org. https://iapp.org/media/pdf/resource_center/Guide_to_Anonymisation.pdf

---

Data Access Monitoring and Reporting

As noted in the callout, data access monitoring is a capability that can be utilized to manage and report on data access and manipulation. As data security has become a higher priority to organizations, new tools are being developed that enable more proactive monitoring of database access, utilizing and going beyond the capabilities of typical database logs. As new tools and capabilities are continually being added to the landscape, we won't attempt to list potential vendors. But some of the capabilities to consider include:

- Monitor and audit all database activity across a variety of database systems
- Enforce separation of duties of database administrators

- Store audit logs and activity reports securely
- Ensure service accounts only access the database from a defined source IP
- Generate alerts when policy violations occur
- Monitor access behavior for anomalies
- Monitor access to sensitive data

Reference

Gartner. *Database Activity Monitoring (DAM)*. Gartner.com. https://www.gartner.com/en/information-technology/glossary/database-activity-monitoring-dam

Cyral. *Database Activity Monitoring (DAM)*. Cyral.com. https://cyral.com/glossary/database-activity-monitoring/

Satori. *Database Activity Monitoring (DAM)*. Satori. https://satoricyber.com/glossary/dam-database-activity-monitoring/

Immuta. *Unified Audit*. Immuta. https://www.immuta.com/product/unified-audit/

Part III

Ongoing Activities

There are ongoing activities that are an integral part of data governance. Chapters 17 and 18, covering Evangelize, Monitor, Report, and Evaluate, remind us that data governance work doesn't end. This may be frustrating to both practitioners and managers, but this reflects the expectation that data needs will always change as both the internal and external business environment changes and evolves. Additionally, it provides job security to experienced data governance professionals.

CHAPTER 17

Evangelize

One of the most important aspects of data governance, like project management, is communication. Sharing information about data governance is as much a part of the job as implementing tools, creating business glossaries, and documenting the data dictionary. Without good communications, organizational team members won't know the data governance standards and expectations, which they are expected to create, manage, handle, view, and share. Team members will not be aware of the tools that are being implemented to improve their ability to interact with and take advantage of the power of organizational data. Management of the data governance organization and executives in other areas of the business will not be aware of the tools and capabilities that are now available to help them reduce risk, add value, and leverage data to create new business opportunities. Communication of data governance concepts should be treated like an ongoing marketing program.

In his books on Guerrilla Marketing, Jay Conrad Levinson stated that research showed that a consumer often required as many as 16 exposures to a product before he or she acted on any interest. We should treat data governance concepts this way. Take every opportunity that allows the team or management to discuss data governance. As we have seen, data governance affects many aspects of the business. For example, data privacy and inadvertent data disclosure training is an opportunity to share information about data governance.

Other training opportunities exist at most organizations, including lunch-and-learn sessions, town hall programs, intranet sites, email distributions, etc. Training formats include live demonstrations, recorded training, computer-based training (CBT), or one-on-one conversations. Program activities create many opportunities for team members to share the goals and objectives of the data governance program with stakeholders. While collecting information for data definitions, the business glossary, or shared data sets, the team can speak about the other tools and information being made available by the program. During these meetings and workshops, subject matter experts can be polled about their challenges and interests related to data governance information, controls, and programs. There are often challenges underlying daily work that can be at least be improved by implementing aspects of data governance. For example, many analysts and technologists have databases that are not cataloged. Technical metadata can often be read into the data catalog to allow at least technical structures to be read. Frequently, we find Excel documents with definitions of data and business terms. These can all be replaced by a central data catalog.

Again, get out and talk to people across the organization about data governance! First, teach them about data governance, data standards, data handling expectations, etc. Then, we want to encourage interest and excitement about the tools and new capabilities, controls being implemented, and information being gathered and made available. Then, we want to encourage participation and input. I've frequently heard comments like "we should do this or that" about the data and its security, control, or documentation. Here's where we must have a chance to gather further needs from the organization. We can use this process to encourage more participation, assuming that we can incorporate those requests back into the program. Incorporating user needs into the risk/value matrix into the next round of improvements will encourage more participation over time.

Reference

Levinson, Jay Conrad. (2007). Guerrilla Marketing. Houghton Mifflin.

CHAPTER 18

Monitor, Report, and Evaluate

A t this point, you've worked through your data governance risk/value matrix and started some activities related to the highest value or highest risk data sets within the organization. As work and time move forward, you should start measuring progress.

> Over the years, I've realized that what doesn't get measured and reported to management didn't happen.

Additionally, you need to understand what aspects of the program are progressing, what aspects add value, and which are just stalled or not making a difference to the organization. Therefore, we need to implement measurement systems to establish whether goals are achieved and how much value or risk avoidance is achieved.

Since many business measurement systems can be useful and may be incorporated into your organization already, I'm not going to recommend any one approach, but I will recommend some aspects of data governance that should be used to show value. Note that identifying value-based measurements for data governance activities can be quite challenging. While it is easy to count how many business terms we've added to the glossary or how many tables and columns have been added to the data catalog, those counts do not readily identify value or risk avoidance.

I recommend going back to your risk and value matrix to identify measurements that reflect the underlying needs of the organization. Additionally, identifying metrics that accurately measure risk avoidance and efficiencies can be very difficult. How do we measure not incurring data loss and the reputational fallout? How do we measure the time users have saved by quickly looking up the source of a particular field, the meaning of a business phrase, or the business term that defines a column in a table? We can create approximations of these measures, but management may remain skeptical.

> *As we develop our approach and identify the data governance functions we plan to implement, we need to be mindful of the goals we plan to achieve and how we plan to measure and report on those goals.*

Here's where we can identify and apply SMART goals. As we develop our approach and identify the data governance functions we plan to implement, we need to be mindful of the goals we plan to achieve and how we plan to measure and report on those goals. For instance, creating a business glossary is not just about adding as many business terms and acronyms to our centralized glossary as possible, but it's about sharing that glossary with staff members who need it. There are various steps along the way to creating and publishing a useful business glossary:

- Identify, document, and publish business terms and acronyms

- Publicize the glossary across the organization to encourage input and user engagement

- Measure usage and involvement in the glossary

- Measure user satisfaction with the glossary.

While the implementation team may feel that the main job is creating the glossary and adding terms and acronyms, the job is not complete. I would argue that the job is never complete because data governance is an ongoing process, not a one-and-done project. More to the point, creating the business term repository is just the start of the work. Now, users must know it exists. They need to start using it. They need to contribute to the glossary. This is where our previous discussion on evangelizing data governance comes into play. Then, we need to understand whether users find the glossary to be helpful, accurate, and worth recommending to others. Each step along the path can be measured. Counting business terms is easy but doesn't get to the heart of the matter, adding value. Creating SMART goals can be challenging, but it provides a more robust foundation to communicate value to management. After all, they are the ones who need to believe in our work and ask for funding to continue or expand it.

As an example, we'll apply SMART goals to our business glossary.

- **Specific:** We want to create a business glossary that provides organizational access to a list of terms used by various departments across the organization. Users of this glossary may include new employees, business and data analysts, technology staff, and management when they either begin working in a new subject area or need to understand the language used by others within the organization. This glossary should initially cover business terms used by sales and marketing team members, expanding to other teams over time.

- **Measurable:** The glossary should include terms that are related to the listed sales and marketing systems. By year-end, we plan to advertise the glossary enough that 50% of technical sales and marketing personnel are aware of the tool. We expect that the initial set of terms will be used by at least 20% of employees over the next year. We hope to achieve a favorability rating of terms in the glossary and the glossary itself of 4 out of 5 in the first year.

- **Assignable**: The data governance team will implement the business glossary with support from the sales and marketing technical team and subject matter experts.

Management will communicate support and enthusiasm for the implementation to encourage use.

- **Realistic:** Note that the specifications, timelines, and numeric goals are limited.

- **Time-related:** Note that the timelines are specific.

Changing Course

In data governance, as in many aspects of business, the environment changes, business needs change, and external pressures require goal adjustments. In my experience, this often involves the impact of other projects or activities on the availability of necessary support and resources to the data governance implementation. For example, external pressures require that technical resources be limited and focused on implementing associated data repositories. Subject matter experts are also involved in high-immediacy projects. This can limit progress in related areas.

In some cases, progress can continue by working with people more efficiently, asking for more management support for resource availability, or simplifying and slowing work efforts. But at some point, it may become necessary to stop working in one area and move to something else. For example, the catalog product vendor may be implementing updates that are not yet available, and the team must wait a few months to utilize these new capabilities. Fortunately, there is always more data governance work ready to switch to. Here again, it is important to have identified goals and metrics, measure progress, and identify stalled projects.

Next Steps

Having measurements and results available after a period of work, say every three to six months, allows the team to identify those areas that have more potential or need more work in the next period. Here, I recommend returning to your risk/value matrix and identifying the next highest-value group of data sets or the next set of functions to add to high-value data sets. Adding results and notes about each period of effort can enhance the matrix and grow information for each data set. I also recommend including information about achieved value. The business environment will have changed since the last review of the risk/value matrix, so any changes should be noted, with ratings adjusted to identify the next high-priority dataset and governance functionality. Monitor progress on DG initiatives. If it's not working or progressing, make changes or move to the next initiative.

Conclusion

I wrote this book because I was unable to find similar information elsewhere. There are many books about data management and data governance, but few about how to approach the topic in a tactical manner. My approach is not perfect and will not be precisely what you need in your organization. However, it provides a way to identify the highest priority data governance work efforts. It provides guidance on creating a data governance program that adds value to your organization and creates progress. My goal here has been to recommend progress rather than falling into analysis paralysis. As in many areas of technology, business needs and tools will move forward more quickly than we imagine. If we focus on adding value based on current knowledge and current status, we can always make changes later.

Unless the world changes significantly, technology and business needs will change before we can document perfect requirements for the data governance organization, data catalog, data standards, data quality, and other aspects of our functions. This is also part of the fun of being in technology right now. Change is happening quickly. Now, this change is driven by AI. Next year, AI may be combined with other technologies or societal change. When the internet started to become a part of everyday use, we didn't know what uses would be made of it. We don't know what AI will provide now. However, we do know that within organizations, data governance will be imperative to using AI well. This includes not only the governance component but also data enablement.

Data governance is a process, not a single project. This is both challenging and exciting.

I recommend the following approach to implementing tactical data governance:

- Start a data set inventory identifying the most important data within your organization.

- Identify the risks and value opportunities associated with these data sets.

- Identify the data governance functions that can be applied to avoid the risks or support the value opportunities you've identified.

- Learn more about the data governance functions, create more detailed inventories of data set details, analyze the data sets where applicable, start the work, and review and measure results.

- Communicate, measure, and evangelize the importance of both the governance and the enablement aspects of data governance.

- Re-evaluate and reset your approach when necessary.

Most importantly, I recommend getting started on governance activities rather than waiting to create the perfect set of requirements or the perfect organizational chart of roles and responsibilities. It is unlikely that any canned program will be perfect for your organization. Additionally, it is unlikely that your team will be aware of all the nuances of data, data usage, and organizational dynamics existing in your organization before you start. Moving forward with aspects such as data quality analysis, creating a data catalog, and documenting externally shared data or other functions will provide a better understanding of the actual data challenges in the organization, will provide stakeholders with something to respond to, and will, if approached in a prioritized manner, start providing value to the organization.

After some progress has been made, adjustments can follow. Your team may decide to invest in a tool that provides more capabilities on one or more aspects of your program. For example, you may find that master data management is a huge challenge, resulting in lost customers, lost marketing opportunities, or regulatory issues. In this case, you may want to invest in a master data management tool for one or more subject areas. Or you may find that the organization has a bigger data quality issue than expected. In this case, it might make sense to implement a toolset that provides strong data profiling capabilities, allows complex data quality analytics, and enables users and analysts to identify and resolve data quality issues.

Index

www.ingramcontent.com/pod-product-compliance
Lightning Source LLC
Chambersburg PA
CBHW071239050326
40690CB00011B/2188